G000245335

Recipe for Success

Recipe for Success

*The ingredients of a
profitable food business*

Karen Green

Matador
9 Priory Business Park,
Wistow Road, Kibworth Beauchamp,
Leicestershire. LE8 0RX
Tel: 0116 279 2299
Email: books@troubador.co.uk
Web: www.troubador.co.uk/matador
Twitter: @matadorbooks

ISBN 978 178803 926 0

British Library Cataloguing in Publication Data.
A catalogue record for this book is available from the British Library.

Printed by CPI, Croyden, UK Ltd
Typeset in 12pt Bembo by Troubador Publishing Ltd, Leicester, UK

Matador is an imprint of Troubador Publishing Ltd

To Mum, who encouraged my love of food
by letting me make mud pies in the garden,
and Dad, who taught me about
retail and gave me my first job, folding jumpers!

Acknowledgements

Mindy Gibbons Klein – www.thebookmidwife.com – without whom this book would not have been possible. She has coached and encouraged me through the challenges of getting this book published.

Ann Griffiths – my mentor at Boots and ongoing inspiration for her ability to create and lead great businesses.

David Sables – www.sentinelmc.com – for teaching me the art of negotiation and reassuring me that my suspicions about the retailers' negotiation techniques were true!

Serena Hibbett – Grow Your Own Marketing – for supporting me through many of my client projects and applying her structured intelligent approach to category marketing and my more helicopter view.

Natalie Sissons – www.suitcaseentrepeneur.com – for inspiring me to relocate to France and having my semi-location independent business.

Lina Mookerjee – www.praxis-ppd.com – my first yoga teacher and enabling me to explore my spiritual side.

Andy Wilkinson – MD of ichiban UK who enabled me to lead my commercial team and contribute to turning the business to profit.

Contents

Contents

Introduction – Why did I write this book?

I went for years not finishing anything. Because, of course, when you finish something, you can be judged.

Erica Jong

As the quote above says, when you finish something you can be judged and nothing is more transparent than an Amazon review. So, it has taken me a while to get started and what actually qualifies me to write this book? Well, apart from a degree in management science where I studied retail marketing, not much academically – but absolute spade-loads in terms of experience. So, what's my story?

The early years – my introduction to retail

I was born into retailing. My father was the manager of a department store in Newbury and in those days, the department store was the hub of the retail high street. And my mother created the illustrations for their Christmas campaigns.

Every year, loads of beautiful things would come home

for my mother to draw – exotic perfume bottles in cut crystal glass, colourful silk scarves and butter-soft leather gloves in exquisite packaging. I adored that time of year and often, despite there not being much money around, one of the beautiful things I admired, would make its way into my Christmas stocking.

As I got older, I continued the family tradition and started in the department store as a Saturday girl at fourteen. I learnt to fold jumpers with a precision which has stayed with me and an eye for all hangers facing the same way – James Gulliver coined the phrase "retail is detail" and so I learnt! I was also taught that the customer is always right and was expected to be charming and accommodating – a useful skill in my later life dealing with the grocers!

My first encounter with Tesco – when they were still no 2

I went to university in Manchester and began a course of BSc Mathematics and Management Science. By the end of the first year, my tutor said I would need to spend all summer studying and working on the mathematics if I were to gain a decent degree. I thought about this for a while and took the path of least resistance and gave up the maths! This may not be a good moral for a book of this kind but it does underpin one of my fundamental beliefs of people management – focus on their strengths not the weaknesses. So, I studied marketing and buyer behaviour, left with a respectable degree and joined Tesco as a marketing graduate trainee working in Terry Leahy's team. My first boss, Mike

Coupe (currently CEO of Sainsbury's) had just arrived from Unilever as a fresh-faced marketeer and we worked together on the sector of eggs, fish and poultry. It was an interesting couple of years and I had many great experiences. I flew in my first aeroplane to Scotland to visit a fish factory – yes, the shiny-faced assistant buyer of twenty-one who thought she knew everything and I spent my twenty-first birthday in Malton Bacon Factory at my first abattoir trying not to cry as the pigs were being slaughtered.

But being ambitious and wanting to do "proper" marketing, I left after two years and went to start a career with Boots that lasted fourteen years. I began as assistant brand manager and thought I had died and gone to heaven! Leaving behind the 4am starts in Grimsby Fish Market and moving to work with advertising and PR agencies who took me to long lunches in very expensive restaurants. Money was no object in the late Eighties and it was a lot of fun. I learnt a lot about brand marketing but I missed the breadth of retail so I returned to my roots, never to return to pure brand management.

I spent many happy years as a food buyer – mostly buying vitamins where my passion for nutrition and healthy eating began. I learnt lots of negotiation techniques for shaking money out of the money tree of suppliers which would not be considered acceptable now but I did well, driving margins up and getting substantial contributions to marketing and promotional funds. I had some great suppliers who were good to me and we launched some fantastic products. My boss said I was the best buyer she had ever had – and we did exceptionally well. She became my first real mentor and I learnt many things from her about being tough, creative and building the right team around me. She led me from buying to selling and then honing my skills as head of new product development for dental. I learnt a lot in those roles about people management, product development strategy and retailer strategy. More of that later!

Moving into food – real food that is!!

After fourteen years with Boots, I knew I would either stay there until retirement or take the lovely redundancy money and follow my dreams of working in the food industry. My husband thought I was mad – leaving a secure job with a good pension for nothing. I had no job to go to but with a pot of cash, I decided it would be just fine and with rash enthusiasm and two young children, I jumped ship. Part of the redundancy deal was an outplacement package which was absolutely fantastic – I learnt so much about how to look for a job, CV writing skills, interview techniques – and it has held me in good stead throughout my life.

I began my commercial life, first in fizzy pop, and then moving finally into real food – ready meals, salads, Christmas puddings and turkeys. My emphasis was largely on own label which allowed me to develop my love of new product development and, occasionally, to indulge my love of food, being paid to go to Michelin-starred restaurants! I discovered I was good at developing new products and winning new business through strong category strategies. However, I also faced the black art of retailers' negotiation techniques from the other side of the table and it was not so great! Being called for meetings at 4pm on a Friday and then the buyer walking out after five minutes, threatening to complain to my boss and have me sacked. Then, very sadly, watching a business that had risen literally from the ashes go into administration because I couldn't get our customers to agree inflationary price increases. I had a lot to learn and learn I did!

The light bulb moment!!

They were immensely difficult and stressful times and I was ready to throw in the towel but being by then a single mother with two young children to support, I persevered and was lucky enough to meet a man called David Sables who runs Sentinel Management. I went on one of their negotiation courses and I saw the light. He uses ex-buyers from the UK grocery retailer base and all the things I thought might be true about how the buyers use psychological techniques to constantly undermine the account manager were true. They told tales of how the buyer would complain about an account manager and have them sacked because "they weren't doing a good job" when in fact they were doing such a great job and they wanted them replaced with a less aggressive, weaker version! And the point of this? Were they all psychopaths? Of course not – it was to shake the money tree that I had so ably shaken as a buyer five years previously. And sure enough, the suppliers (and these were big branded houses) would hand over cash – in many different forms: promotional support, margin improvements, etc., etc.

Well, for me that was the "light bulb" moment that people talk about – I learnt the techniques on that course some of which I still use today and reference in this book. I took that learning to my final "proper" job – commercial director at an own-label sushi manufacturer. There I pushed through inflationary increases, developed some amazing products, grew the category and built a strong and powerful team. I will reference that a lot in the book as I am proud of the work we did and there are a lot of learnings for us all.

Now

After my children left to go to university, I decided it was time for freedom and change and so relocated to the south of France. I set up my website www.foodmentor.co.uk and my new business was born, mentoring food producers and entrepreneurs. I spent three years working with The Prince's Trust as a business mentor and am a guest lecturer at As Nottingham Trent University teaching about commercial aspects of the food industry. I love the variety of what I do and the opportunity to make a difference to enable people to take charge of their food businesses and to love what they do.

To help support this, I have taken all my learnings and experiences in food and retailing and put them into this book. I want to help other food businesses build their powerbase, enable them to work with retailers and grow lean and nimble businesses that can adapt to the changing retail landscape.

So what are you going to get from reading this?

- Ability to analyse your business to know where its opportunities for growth and improvement lie
- Learn how to design profitable products that will underpin your brand and sell... lots!
- Get to know your customer – their needs, wants and desires and how you can fulfil them
- How to sell successfully into retailers and negotiate a great deal
- How to keep the f***-up fairy at bay and avoid some of the pitfalls
- How to keep evolving your business to grow and beat the competition year after year

And most importantly of all :

- How to have the best fun in the world – because the food industry is awesome and I love it!!

Section 1

Where are you now?

Chapter 1 Stress, distress and success of running a food business

Success is not final; failure is not fatal: it is the courage to continue that counts.

Winston Churchill

Over the past thirty-five years that I have been in retail, the world has changed greatly. The retailers dominate the retail landscape. Tesco has 28% market share of UK grocery but no brand has more than 1% – power is in their hands. £1 out of every £8 spent in the UK is spent in Tesco!!!

The consumer has changed greatly over the years. He/ she is now a shopper in charge of the decision-making process far more than ever. Brands do not hold the same dominant position that they once did – so what's changed?

Massive proliferation:

- Number of products on offer – there are so many more leading brands, challenger brands and own label. Coconut water started out as new in 2004 launched by

Vitacoco – closely followed by a number of challenger brands; and then the big boys such as Innocent and retailer brands had offered variations. Indeed, the Innocent brand itself wrote the definitive book (in reality it's great – *A Book About Innocent*) on how to launch a smoothie brand and it dominated the market until the own-label boys developed alternatives. And then, challenger brands such as Savse, found niches within the category that Innocent had effectively created – nipping away at Innocent's dominant position creating a £10m brand of their own.

- Number of ways of shopping – when I began my career at Tesco in 1986, we had about 350 stores. Now there are over 3,500 in the UK alone, not to mention overseas – and these are subdivided into Superstores, Express, Metro, online, etc. As I write, they are also in the process of bidding for Booker which will add further complexity to the offer. And this is just classic retail – there is also the growth of Amazon, home delivery, meal kits such as Hello Fresh, etc., etc. Just Eat turned over £370m in 2017 purely from delivering other outlets' takeaways.

- Ways of promoting – when I was young, there was only TV in the afternoon and evening and only three channels – BBC1, BBC2 and ITV. Now I believe there are over a thousand on my free sat box. As a brand manager, there were four ways we would promote a product – TV advertising, press advertising, PR and in-store promotions. Now, of course, there is the development of social media, and the ability to reach the customer with your message, becomes infinitely more complex. Once, we would just advertise on mass media and hope someone read it. John Wanamaker said "I know half my advertising works but I don't know which half!". But now you have the ability to target your message to one specific person, or ten or twenty.

- Growth of private label – there are some markets that reign supreme on brand and we will look more at this in Chapter 5. But suffice to say that over 50% grocery is private label although the growth has reversed over the last couple of years.

- Paradox of choice – the change in buyer behaviour. When I was at university, I did a whole module on the psychology of how people buy and how to make it more effective. There are more and more books written on this subject and also the paradox of choice and information overload. The consumer is in charge. She doesn't have to rely on the advice of the local shopkeeper – which was just that: local and biased! Remember the BBC's *Open All Hours* programme where Ronnie Barker's fabulous Arkwright was always coming up with creative schemes to sell more products? Now there are online reviews to discover the best products, mysupermarket.com to find the best price and numerous other ways to inform and enable the customer. There is a wealth of information to turn the buyer into a true shopper – informed and able – and yet so overwhelmed by all that knowledge and the paradox of choice. I think this is why John Lewis is so successful – other than its inspirational Christmas adverts about penguins and trampolining dogs, of course. You can still go and shop there safe in the knowledge that their staff are well trained to help you find the best product and "Never knowingly undersold" means you don't need to worry about the price – an easy shop.

So, what does that mean to you working in food businesses, trying to make a success and make your profitable way through?

YOU NEED HELP!! And here it is, in the form of this book – which you may have bought in a paperback, downloaded as an e-book or even listened to as an audio version – the paradox of choice personified! I have written this book for you.

Before we get into the detail of the book, I want you to think about the three possible outcomes for your business which form the title of this Chapter – stress, distress or success?

Which one do you want to choose for your business?? I have lived through all three with different clients over the years and want to ensure that once you have finished reading this book you have the plan for only one – success – hence the name of the book – *Recipe for Success*. But let's think about the other two first!

Stress

The definition of stress is "a state of mental or emotional strain or tension resulting from adverse or demanding circumstances" *English Oxford Living Dictionary*. I often use the definition that it is the feeling of not being in control – pressure is great and stimulating but when it overwhelms then it becomes harmful.

It is likely you are reading this and nodding your head at this point and saying that IS the food industry. By its very nature of being fast and dynamic, there are going to be high pressure moments and these can be stimulating and rewarding. Many people in the food industry love the adrenalin rush, the need to solve problems and the high of success (myself included!).

But real stress is when you can't cope with the rain of pressure and then it becomes a medically bad thing.

Everyone knows when they are stressed – can't sleep, always tired, more headaches than normal (certainly true in my case). Maybe you dream about the particular situation. Sometimes you extrapolate and lose all sight of reality – I know I certainly have on several occasions in my life where I am not in control of the situation and a retailer is threatening to delist, we have a product recall or total inability to supply.

And what are the things we worry about?

- Losing business
- Falling out with key customers (and the potential of lost business)
- Product recalls
- Bad press coverage
- Business going into distress (see next section!)

- Personal impact – maybe getting sidelined from promotion or worse, getting sacked!

All of these are caused by fear of failure and often a lack of structure in the business to cope with the challenges that life throws at us. When I worked at ichiban, the MD had a catch-all for when things went wrong – and called it the "f***-up fairy". I absolutely loved the description because it was said with a degree of sarcasm and cynicism, i.e. he meant how has this particular situation occurred without our being in control of the situation. Had some magical fairy come down and just created havoc or actually was it the fault of the managers who had missed some critical control point or understanding of the situation that had meant a disaster had ensued? After a few months working with the business, implementing new systems, putting in the right people to run them, the fairy did not visit so often – but she is definitely very stressful and in Chapter 11, we look at how you can protect against her!

Distress

When I started writing this book, I had never heard of the phrase "distress" being an actual term for a company that is struggling and in danger of bankruptcy. Begbies Traynor specialises in helping distressed companies and publish quarterly numbers for various industries including food. In Q4 2016, UK's food and beverage manufacturing industry, which supplies the major UK supermarkets, showed a 13% increase in "significant" distress over the past year, with 5,986 businesses now struggling, compared to 5,312 at the same stage last year. The research indicates that small suppliers have been most affected, with SMEs making up 94% of companies in distress within the sector. That's a lot of people like you and me sitting at their desk worrying about what is going to happen to their business.

The key indicators of distress are as follows:

- Decreased profits – common in the current climate of inflation, Brexit, increased living wage and other financial pressures
- Falling sales volumes and losing market share – possibly losing to other more nimble brands/suppliers and/or trading in a declining market
- Pay cuts and freezes – apart from, of course, the ever-increasing living wage
- Loss of regular customers
- Cash flow difficulties – suppliers insisting on proforma invoices. This can be a difficult situation not just for businesses in distress but also start-ups – both of whom may have poor credit ratings
- Redundancies and loss of key personnel as people realise that the business is not doing well
- Factoring invoices to try and support cash flow – many small businesses use factoring to enable them to overcome cash-flow difficulties but when the average food company net profit % is about 5% then giving away 2–3% is a significant amount to give away unless you need that cash flow
- Borrowing to pay off existing debt

CASE STUDY

The company – I was working with a frozen food company in the North-East who had previously been in administration and had been given a new lease of life with new owners. The workforce worked tirelessly on their factory, rebuilding it from the ashes literally as it had suffered a fire. They developed new products, sold them into both retailers and brand owners and had a factory that achieved a positive audit on its first attempt. We had a great management team and quality products.

The problem – there were two issues surrounding profitability and consequential cash flow. The products had not been costed properly and the customer agreements had very long notice periods. Disaster struck as the two key ingredients – wheat and beef, the two key components of this company's production – went through the roof in terms of inflation. I tried to override the customer agreements and negotiate through price increases but they were rejected.

Slowly the focus of the management team changed – we were managing supply, not on orders, but on what raw materials we had available. Some suppliers continued to be supportive but others moved on to proformas. We factored invoices to try and improve cash flow and spent our focus prioritising payment.

The solution – sadly, our first case study of the book does not end happily. The situation did not improve and the business went into administration, leaving many workers out of a job and many creditors out of pocket (including myself).

It was a horrible experience and I learnt many things about contract negotiation, product design and resilience at pushing through inflation – the sad thing is that the retailer who would not put up their cost prices for us, was forced to move to another supplier and in less than two months their retail prices went up by 30%.

One of the book's key purposes is to help you avoid ever getting into the situation of distress and if you do get into trouble, as risks need to be taken, you will know how to find your way out again. Which leads us on to the happy place of success…

Success

So how do you avoid the stress and distress of the failing business and experience the joy of success of an evolving, profitable one?

Knowing it is running like clockwork with profitable products flying off the shelf and happy retailers and consumers alike! I developed the POWER model of success:

P – Product

The most important element of your business. Your business needs to sell great food that meets the needs of your consumer. Those needs may change but if you have an amazing product then retailers will want to stock you and customers will want to eat it. It is not always that simple, of course, as the needs of consumers change, competitors come and steal from your category, products come in and out of fashion and your once cheap commodity that you made it with becomes unbearably expensive. However, if you can take charge of your product offering, you are halfway home to taking charge of your business – we talk a lot about this in Chapters 5 and 6 and then the challenge of evolving to meet the market needs in Chapter 13.

CASE STUDY

The company – one product that I believe is pretty unique and has stood the test of time is Marmite. I talk a lot about Marmite in this book as I believe it is, in some ways, the perfect brand that has stood the test of time. It evolved as a by-product of the brewing industry being launched in Burton-on-Trent where there were a number of brewers and a lot of brewer's yeast! It has a unique packaging shape and a name that references the pot and not the actual product. Maybe if it had been assessed in research, it would not have come to market as it is so polarising, yet they have used the "love it or hate it" theme in the advertising for over ten years.

The problem – how to keep evolving. The product is named after the shape of the packaging and let's be honest, there is only one Marmite recipe!! No one has yet developed smoked BBQ Marmite or an avocado version!!

The solution – innovation around the edges!! The parent packaging has remained unchanged but there have been a number of customer-orientated changes e.g. squeezy bottles and little pots for the catering market (both Marmite shaped) or a variety of licensing opportunities – from crisps to chocolate.

So, they haven't changed the product, just accepted its uniqueness and the phrase "something/someone is like Marmite" is now widely used. And due to this uniqueness, it commands a high price despite Marmite-gate, when Tesco and Unilever fell out over inflationary increases. It actually breaks some of the rules/suggestions that we make later in the book that you should meet customer needs – it is exceptionally high in salt but perceived as high in B vitamins so it is almost a health food, plus half the population hates it! Find another Marmite and to my mind, you have found product nirvana.

O – Organisation

When a business first starts up, there is usually an entrepreneur who has an idea and begins making it in their shop or on the kitchen table. They do all the work and then slowly begin to evolve, bringing in help. From there, the organisation will grow to meet the needs of the business organically until sometimes you have a complex structure that is unwieldy and complicated. The business targets may not all be aligned and people may have forgotten the point of what they are trying to achieve.

Similarly, the type of people a business needs will change and grow as the direction and strategy of the business evolve. So, taking the recipe for success of your food business means making sure your organisation is well structured, focused and well led which we will examine in Chapter 10. The people need to be well chosen to meet the needs of today and be invested in to enable them to evolve for the needs of tomorrow.

W – Well-being

Well-being is a strange one to suddenly introduce in amongst all this management speak but it is one for me that has been key to my success and survival during the tough days of f***-up fairies and difficult retailer conversations when the stress is high and joy is low.

It is critical to think about how you look after yourself as an individual – knowing yourself and how to take care of your well-being is paramount to success. There are many studies that show that people perform better when they are well rested, well nourished, fit and healthy. It is kind of obvious but not always thought about in the business context. And similarly, not just your personal well-being but also that of your staff. It is no coincidence that larger companies offer gyms on site, free gym membership and yoga classes in the lunch break. A team at the peak of its health and fitness will take much better charge than one that is exhausted surviving on little sleep and rubbish food.

E – Evolution

As discussed in the beginning of this section, we will focus on how to keep a business evolving in Chapter 13. It is a critical part of any business to keep understanding the changing needs of the customer and adapting product offer accordingly.

But not just the product… the organisation, marketing, even legislation, etc. The world is so fast moving you have to keep up and your business needs to evolve with it.

R - Results

I have talked about the need for a well-aligned team with focus on the same end game and nothing is more important to get results. Chapter 11 talks about what type of targets you need to set and how to monitor them. How can you know if you are doing well if you don't have a detailed breakdown of your profit margin by product possibly by day or at least by month?

Some products don't have a variable cost – the line is set up and it runs off a batch and that is that. However, if you take sushi as an example, the profit can vary by day and by season due to the volume variations – more sales on a Monday as people are being healthy and more in the height of summer and the lowest ebb at Christmas. The cost of the product doesn't really change in terms of raw materials but the labour costs vary as the efficiency of the lines changes with less product made per shift.

It is important to understand the drivers of your products' costs and potential risks – currency/inflation, etc.

But it doesn't just have to be financial numbers – quality, supply and even staff absence can all be measured and quantified.

You need systems in place to do the measuring and people who are brought into the targets so that they know why they are working with them and how they are going to help make their life easier.

So, in summary, this book sets out to find the recipe for success and how to avoid the stress and distress of running a food business and to give some insights into how to create success and enjoy being part of an amazing, stimulating industry.

Exercise

Divide a piece of paper into two (or use two PowerPoint slides or Pinterest boards or whatever is your thing) and list out in words, draw pictures or use photos and build your model of:

- what success looks, sounds and feels like
- what stress and distress look, sound and feel like

for you. It is good to have something that you want to go towards and something you definitely want to work away from to help motivate you when times get tough and the f***-up fairy comes.

So, now you have your vision and what's going to feel good; we had better find out where you are now – in Chapter 2.

Chapter 2 Knowing the business and you

If you don't know where you want to go, then it doesn't matter which path you take.

Lewis Carroll *Alice in Wonderland*

There is an old joke about the Irishman who is asked for directions and he says, "Well, I am not sure of the way but I certainly wouldn't start here!" Most clients that I work with find they do not have a good understanding of where they are, let alone where they want to be. In fact, in many cases, they have a better vision of where they would like to be, i.e. increased sales, better cash flow, making a profit and yet when I ask for a breakdown by line of their sales, profitability, etc., they struggle.

With all my clients, I begin with an informal audit process to understand where the challenges lie and hence the opportunities. We then look at the numbers to see what information is available and what will need work/estimates. Sometimes information just isn't forthcoming and so you have to use your experience and find another way to fill in the blanks.

So, here's your opportunity to understand your business and take the following audit. You may need to take it for several different parts of your business – for example, your business may operate in more than one category and some of it may not apply. Add up the numbers at the end and give yourself a score out of 17 (you get bonus points depending on your customer relationships). At the end, I will go through each question and give examples of how you can use the audit to make a success plan.

The food business audit

Score 1 for yes and 0 for no.

		YES	NO
1.	Do you measure sales/profit on at least a monthly basis?		
2.	Is your category or market in growth?		
3.	Does your brand/own-label offer have a strong share – e.g. over 20%?		
4.	Do you have a defined understanding of your key customer base?		
5.	Is your consumer loyal?		
6.	Factory – is your factory well invested and does it have a good BRC/SALSA score?		
7.	Have you lost a customer recently or had a bad renegotiation of terms?		
8.	Are there fewer than three or four competitors in your marketplace?		
9.	Do you have more than three or four major customers?		
10.	Is your product made up of a few components?		

Score zero also if you are very dependent on specific commodities, e.g. wheat for pasta supplier, salmon for sushi company, etc.		
11. Do you have strong people in each of your key customer-facing areas, e.g. sales/ national accounts, category, new product development, technical?		
12. Do you have positive feedback from your customers? Score zero if you have not proactively sought feedback!		
13. Is your range of products high performing in terms of product quality, category knowledge and innovation?		
14. Review the following definition and choose the one that best describes your retailer relationships – score zero for bronze, 1 for silver and 2 for gold.		
– Bronze – new listings and negotiations are based mostly on price and other financial deals		
– Silver – we are partners with the retailer, building category plan for the year together		
– Gold – we are partners with up to five years' worth of plans with mutually beneficial joint ventures and long-term commitment		
15. Are your teams happy and productive with low absenteeism and staff turnover?		
16. Cash flow – is your cash flow positive (score zero if you are relying on factoring, borrowing to pay off debts or reliant on overdraft).		

The point of this audit is to do two things – one, to identify where your areas of challenge are and secondly, to see overall how strong and powerful you are as a business. Clearly if you score 17, you can sit back, pop the book in the bin and feel happy that you are in charge of your business. But even if you have a low score, it will show where your areas of strength are and this is really important when you are negotiating both with retailers and suppliers as we will discover in chapters 7 and 8.

This is not a scientific based audit that has been tested and proven to be an indicator of success or failure. But it is a good summary of the expert views of the key flags for identifying companies in distress and your opinion, whilst a subjective view, is as good as any. Most of us know our business very well – we just need to structure our understanding of where we are and what the future holds.

So, let's take each of the questions in turn:

1. Do you measure your sales and profit on at least a monthly basis? "You can't manage what you can't measure" is a simple but obvious statement and one that needs no introduction – in Chapter 11 we look at setting KPIs – what are good ones and what can sometimes drive bad behaviour.

2. Market growth – a lot of successful businesses flourish in the good times when the market is in massive growth and there are easy wins to be had by growing sales and if there is capacity, this will tend to lead to increased profits due to coverage of overheads. One of my strongest

challenges when I was working with ichiban was that the market had been in double-digit growth and our share of this supplying Tesco, as market leader ,was on the crest of this wave. As the market became saturated and our ready supply of new customers to the marketplace began to dwindle as all those who were going to try sushi had tried it, we were left facing harder times.

This leads us on to the challenge of market share:

3. Market share – if your market share is over 20%, then you are in a very strong position – Tesco totally overtrades in sushi vs their share of total grocery. This put us in a very strong position to totally dominate and lead the market through innovation and newness. Although, if you are dominating a market that is in decline then you are in a more challenging position but own the market and you have power.

4. Do you have a defined understanding of your customer base? Knowing your customer is key – putting the customer at the heart of everything we do is a mantra I have heard from both retailers and brands. But you need to know who he or she is, what are the demographics that define her and psychographics that drive her. More of that in Chapter 3.

5. Consumer loyalty – do you have loyal consumers who come back time and time again for your product or are high users? Clearly this is the holy grail – a product that people absolutely love and will cross the street or town for – for which there is no substitute. In this ever-changing world there are very few products that are

like this. Promiscuity is one of the key drivers of the modern consumer. My favourite example, Marmite, is probably the ultimate in loyalty – if you like Marmite you are devoted – you love it! You can assess loyalty through your social media following, your retailer data and other market analysis.

6. Factory – is your factory well invested?

When I originally wrote this, I was thinking about companies that make their own products or who are own-label suppliers. Many of my clients have manufactured for retailers and the investment in factory infrastructure, training and quality is critical. I did some work for a bakery in London and even on my first tour round the factory I could see there were going to be issues ahead. The floor was cracked, the dust controls were poor and there was an infestation of cockroaches. I was assured by the factory manager that this was quite usual in a bakery and the locality had a very robust strain that were hard to eliminate. Well, suffice to say, when we had a site visit from the key customer, we were red-sited, which, for those of you lucky people who have never had that experience, is a NIGHTMARE – all NPD was instantly stopped but for some reason we were allowed to continue production but under supervision. My visits as a commercial manager to the retailer head office were long and painful.

But this may not apply to you, as some of the most successful companies in the world don't actually make their own products. For example, Innocent drinks,

Coca-Cola – they may have a secret recipe but they have it bottled by a co-packer. If that is the case for your business then in some ways the question may seem less relevant. However, investment is key because you really don't want to have the challenge of finding a new producer, find that your competitors products are more cost effective due to investment in automation or it doesn't comply with the latest quality requirements.

7. Bad customer relationships – if you lost a customer recently or had a bad renegotiation of terms this means that you may not be in the strong position that you are hoping for. Sometimes, loss of a customer can actually improve the bottom line. I had one client for whom I successfully lost a quarter of their key accounts business but it reduced the reliance on that customer and enabled a pruning of lines to enable NPD to grow. We will discuss customers further in chapters 7 and 8.

8. Competition – Porter's model of power in the organisation cites the number of suppliers in the marketplace as a key source of power. If there are only a few alternatives then you are in a strong position. Using the example of the sushi market, there are very few manufacturers, as it is a difficult product to make and is labour-intensive coupled with a high percentage of raw material costs. This means that there are fewer price tenders, fewer price wars and generally fewer downward pressures on price. But sometimes competition IS a good thing, especially in a relatively new market – I often say to my start-up clients, don't be too disheartened if there

25

are other people in the marketplace – it means there is a definite customer need and you can learn from the early prospectors' mistakes. But generally, less competition means more dominance for you.

9. Customer complexity – once again, this is a general rule but it can have exceptions. Ideally a business should be spread successfully across a number of different customers. Proliferation of customer-specific products, e.g. specific pack sizes or outer case sizes can add cost but generally spreading the business, spreads the risk. I worked with a cake company that was 95% one UK retailer and mostly made own label. She was skilled at her production and had a great understanding of the category. Sadly, the retailer took her category ideas, worked with a larger manufacturer who outbid her on price and her business went into administration.

10. Product composition – this is an interesting area and doesn't have to mean that a business will fail if it is just one component as frankly there would be no produce/chicken/fish processors. But they do generally have much lower margins than businesses that are less dependent on raw materials, e.g. Coca-Cola. If you are dependent on specific commodities then you will potentially have a roller coaster of a business – it doesn't mean it won't be profitable if it starts in the right place but it can have a real downward effect on profit. For example, Pip & Nut has found herself in a very difficult position facing massive price increases on almonds, etc. and she is lucky because she has developed a brand

loyalty and price-insensitive following that will enable her to ride out the storm.

11. Strong team of people – if you have a strong, capable team, then you are lucky and should do everything you can to keep them. So much has been written about this subject but with the right people your business is in a much better position than anyone else. They will drive the innovation, the category strategies, ensure your customer is happy and your factory is running well.

12. Customer feedback – by customers I am meaning your retail customers not your consumers (although that is important too). I have recently worked with a client who had had atrocious feedback from their customer – pretty much every single criterion from innovation to account management to service level was in the red. I spent eight months specifically focusing on these elements and getting them from the doldrums whereby they lost a chunk of business back into the green whereby they are now in a position to win new business. The reason I said score 0 for not knowing your customers views is that often if we are not forced into receiving feedback through one of the main UK retailers, we are inclined to put our head in the sand and hope for the best! The manager who is in charge of his/her business will know the customer view, acknowledge and may even choose to ignore it (often at their peril) but at least they know and there shouldn't be any nasty surprises.

13. Good product quality – we will examine in Chapter 12,

how to cope when things go wrong but good product quality is so key. If you have a production facility that produces great quality every day then your waste will be minimised as all production will be good. There will be consistency for your consumers so that they will get the same product that they are expecting every time they buy – except if you are making something artisan where uniqueness is a key selling point! And you avoid the dreaded recall which costs thousands and thousands and in worst case scenarios can kill a brand.

14. Customer relationships – the best relationship that we want with our customers is the silver or gold one – where ideally you are beyond a simple price transaction and adding value on both sides of the relationship. You may be working together to create the future of the category – maybe even creating a joint venture with a factory built just for the retailer. This can happen and is very successful. However, a few years ago there was a factory built for a UK retailer and sadly before it could open the retailer decided to go with another supplier – luckily that was a large and successful manufacturer who managed to fill the capacity with other products but the relationship was certainly never gold from their side again.

Silver is where most of us get to if we are lucky – we have got a joint business plan, we know how we are going to build the category going forward and our new products are on their listing plans. We have some tough negotiations but they are fair and collaborative. The tough one is the bronze level which are very transactional relationships and reflect where many retailers have got to with some of their product areas. They base their listings on price and use tenders to seal the deal – there is not the collaboration and therefore less opportunity to drive the category forwards and upwards. It is more difficult to take charge of these relationships and we will examine it further in Chapter 9. Higher profit margins are harder but not impossible to come by.

15. Happy and productive business culture – you may have a positive answer to number 11 – yes, I have great people but without the right culture, these people will struggle to achieve outstanding performance levels. High absenteeism and staff turnover is a business that is not in charge and is having to deal with filling the gaps of missing people either in the short term due to absenteeism or long term due to having to recruit new people. Chapter 10 will focus on how to maximise the cultural element of your business but it comes from many things – clear targets, positive feedback, space to make mistakes and the feeling of being part of something successful – like your food business!

16. Cash flow – a successful business needs to be in charge of its cash flow to ensure that they do not overpay for money, can buy raw materials, pay wages and generally keep investing in the business. I look more at this in Chapter 13.

So, in conclusion, hopefully you now have an idea of the areas where your business is strong and maybe there are areas that you need to take charge of in more detail.

The business leader audit

Whilst we are on the analysis trail, how about you? How do you feel as a leader, a foodpreneur? – Are you in great shape to get on and lead the business or are you struggling? Seth Godin, in his book *Tribes,* defines elements of leadership which are useful to think about before we audit your leadership style:

- Do you challenge the status quo and have a level of curiosity about your business world?
- Do you have the charisma to motivate people to be led?
- Can you communicate and commit to your vision of what good looks like?

If you can honestly say yes to all these then you are on the way but for more structure have a go at this simple leadership audit:

Score a simple 1 for yes and 0 for no.

		YES	NO
1.	Are you considerate of your teams – give them freedom to act, treat them with respect?		
2.	Do you love the business like it is your own (and indeed it might be!)?		
3.	Do you have the experience to do your role as leader successfully?		

4.	Are you committed to results and achieving them in a structured and timely manner?		
5.	Are you innovative offering team solutions and new ideas?		
6.	Are you team orientated and successful at inspiring others to do their best?		
7.	Do you look after yourself physically – eating well, not too much alcohol and regular exercise?		
8.	Do you sleep well?		
9.	Do you have a strong support network emotionally to give you support outside work?		
10.	Do you have a strong business network to provide knowledge and support and to keep abreast of industry developments?		
11.	Do you invest in yourself and others in terms of personal development?		
12.	Are you confident to do the job as a business leader?		

So how did you do? 12/12 and fighting fit, or struggling with a few of these and in need of a little taking charge of yourself?!

Well, let's run through each question which has been compiled from my experience of successful clients and their leaders.

1. Consideration to your teams – a strong leader will enable the team to do well but also more importantly will treat them with respect. We have talked a little about the f***-up fairy in this book already and when she comes along and waves her wand – do you shout

and blame your team or respect that they are doing their best? I am reminded of "Mrs Do-As-You-Would-Be-Done-By" in Charles Kingsley's *The Water Babies*.

2. Love the business like it is your own – you may be reading this and be a business owner, MD or start-up foodpreneur and to be sure, you will be driven by the love of your business. But you may not be; you may be an employee or working part-time to help a company. Either way, you may love and feel passion for your business or it may have sucked the very life out of you – in which case you may be weary and in need of reinvigoration. Loving the business as your own avoids some of what I call "should-ing". When I hear people say, "they should do this" about the organisation I feel there is a disconnect from the business which needs to be rediscovered to enable successful leadership.

3. Experience levels – experience comes in many forms and only you can judge if you have the experience to do the job. If you are an MD of a larger food company, it is unlikely that you have in-depth experience of all the job functions of the business but you will have experience of leadership and delivery of success. I work with numerous companies in different food industries from Christmas puddings to turkeys to produce but my common theme has been food and UK retail. Some people believe that enough experience means you have been in an industry all your life and some don't. What actually matters is if you think you have enough experience and if not, how you are going to compensate

for that either through learning or bringing in someone who does.

4. Results orientation – when I was at university, I studied occupational and industrial psychology and was fascinated to learn that there were two types of personality defined by Meyer Friedman and Ray Rosenman in the fifties. Type As who are highly motivated, results orientated and on edge to get stuff done (err me!) and Type Bs who are more laid back and easy going. It was a surprise to me at eighteen that not everyone was like me and it took me a lot longer to realise that there is more than one path to achieve results. However, in business we need to create a focus on getting results and also achieving them in a structured and timely manner. Because then other people in the organisation know what they are doing, are aligned and feel better in the organisation. Some just need less structure than others!

5. Innovative thinking – as a leader, we have to be able to think up solutions using our experience and innate creativity that offers inspiration to take the business forward. I am mindful that many entrepreneurs, that I work with, are not short of ideas and innovative thinking and actually the opposite is true; they need to have fewer ideas and repeat the mantra "focus works"!

6. Team orientation – there are two ways to build a team (well, there are probably hundreds but this is my take on it) – you either recruit people who are exactly like you and surround yourself with yes men and sycophants

OR you look deep inside yourself and ask what am I not good at? And then build the team around you to balance the strengths, experience and personalities. In my last major role as commercial director, I got sucked into doing some admin which I am really, really bad at. I made a mistake and as a result, we were involved in a major recall – not a public one fortunately but the one where the retailer has to take the product off the shelves – and you are charged for loss of profit and admin costs – it was the worst week of my working life and I offered to resign. The MD at the time said, "you have added more value whilst you have been here than you have just destroyed so I cannot accept the resignation". That was a very emotional moment for me but there are two learnings there. One, he recognised the breadth of differing skills that I brought to his team and secondly, I needed to balance my skill set and so recruited myself the very best admin person I have ever had. She compensated for my shortfalls and I coached her a lot on hers.

7. Are you in good shape? – I am not expecting to see photos of Adonis foodpreneurs on my Facebook page after reading this but, generally, do you look after yourself? If you are running a health food business you may be radiant with health, practise yoga and repeat the mantra "my body is a temple" every day. OK, just kidding, but really working in the food industry is on full and very demanding so you need to be up to the job. That means well nourished, well exercised and well

rested – all work and no play makes Jonny a dull boy – I know I have done it!

8. Sleep – much has been written on the importance of sleep. In fact, I was reading an article about it today – Donald Trump gets by on about four to five hours a night retiring at 12-1am and getting up again to read the news and reactions to his Twitter feed no doubt at five in the morning. He slated Hillary Clinton for her need for sleep during the election campaign. Margaret Thatcher only needed four hours but would have a zizz in the afternoon and Churchill was similar, taking a cat nap in the afternoon… in pyjamas. Well, I need a good eight hours otherwise I cannot function. If you have a change in your sleep habits and are waking up worrying about business, then all is not well. Be mindful to take care of your rest. There is a great book - *The Sleep Book: How to Sleep Well Every Night* by Guy Meadows which is worth reading to help you if you have a sleep challenge.

9. Emotional support network – I am very lucky to have a good friend who works alongside me with many of my clients who is really, really supportive when I stumble ready to fall. She will listen to my little rants, offer some great advice which brings me back to reality and I can then go back to whatever problem has thrown me off course and I am more effective. I have done the same for her on a couple of occasions. Do you have people outside work who can listen, offer advice if needed or not if just a sounding board is required? It is helpful and therapeutic.

10. Business support network – how many people do you know in the food industry – outside your company? Ten, a hundred, a thousand? How many can you call upon to get some really great advice, who will know other people who may be able to keep you abreast of the industry? When I went through one of the retailers' reset programmes two years ago, I used my network like crazy. I heard what was happening to other companies in my category, in other areas, heard about competitors and generally was much better able to put into perspective what was happening. It was still a stressful and challenging experience but helped by knowing what was happening and it enabled me to do a better job. Working in isolation is when the paranoia can set in.

11. Personal development – an investment or a waste of money? In my last role as commercial director, the only personal development I undertook was to attend IGD conferences. The business was short of money and so personal development, over and above the basic requirements that are necessary for such things as BRC, was seen as an unnecessary cost. But I invested a lot personally in coaching and learning which has proved invaluable. In this ever-changing world we all need to grow and develop to keep up.

12. Confidence – paint a smile on your face and you will be happy. Laugh and the world laughs with you – if you exude confidence then it inspires others. We all have days when we doubt we can do things – think of all the

times I have had a wobble about whether I could write this book. But generally, confidence that you can take charge of your business – usually means you can!

I read an amazing book by Fiona Harrold called *Indestructible self-belief* and still use it now with my clients and myself when I have a wobble!

Exercise

1. Using the business audit, write down a list of the top three areas that you believe you need to focus on in the next month and then work out some key actions as to how you may solve them.

   For example:

	Challenge	Planned solution	Timescales	Who?
1	I don't know my customer well enough	Read chapter 3 Conduct market survey Review social media metrics		
2	My factory is not up to scratch	Lead improvement plan Look for grants/ funding opportunities		
3	I don't have a strong team around me	Read chapter 10 Identify the roles you are missing Write role description and person specification Begin recruiting		

2. Using the personal audit, identify three key areas that you would like to work on to improve your leadership skills, well-being or industry knowledge. Prioritise them just like a business target – your business needs a strong, healthy leader to thrive – make sure it's you!!

Section 2

Taking charge – creating your USP

Chapter 3 Understand your consumer

You will get all you want in life, if you help enough other people get what they want.

Zig Ziglar

The consumer is no longer a simple animal. When I started my career, it was all about demographics – age, sex, social class and no one really looked into the psychographics of behaviour. There was not the paradox of choice, both in terms of retail outlets or products, so life was a little easier for both the marketeer and the consumer herself.

Life has become very paradoxical – let's take the example of music. In the beginning, there was vinyl – you could get a reasonable sound but it was then replaced by the CD which gave much better quality of sound. Then the focus was on how to get the equipment to give the best sound. The CD was then replaced by music downloads and what parent does not now suffer with their children playing music from their phone – poor quality but convenient. And then finally to bring us full circle, vinyl is back in vogue – retro, desirable and expensive but with neither the convenience of download nor the quality of CD.

So, to launch a successful food product and keep it successful you almost need a degree in psychology to understand what the decision-making process is and how to influence it.

There are a few things that you need to know to discover what is truly driving your consumers' behaviour – I call it the who and why.

Who is your customer?

You need to understand who your customer is so that you can ask them what is driving their purchasing decisions.

1. Demographics – age, sex, social class, retailer specific definitions (most retailers have also classified their shoppers into groups which are useful to know), income and marital status. You can analyse this through market data such as Kantar or Nielsen if it is available to you or by looking at your social media engagement – what is the profile of the people who are engaging with your brand.

2. Psychographics – this is understanding your customers' motivations for buying your products in terms of their key interests. Alex Osterwalder in his book *Value Proposition Design: How to Create Products and Services Customers Want* says there are three key tasks that your products can play:

   Jobs – these are the three ways that a product can do a job for the customer:

   – Functional jobs such as feeding the kids or making

sure you have a packed lunch

  – Social jobs which are more about status – your
    food brand may have kudos and social class – e.g.
    shopping at Waitrose for lunch may look better to
    colleagues than home-made cheese and pickle!

  – Personal/Emotional jobs – this is all about feeling
    good – treating yourself to a glass of wine or buying
    that bar of chocolate

3. Pains – how does your product overcome the pain that
    your customer feels. So, for example, that pain may be
    feeling or (actually being) overweight – your product
    can solve this pain by being low fat or low sugar. The
    person who is trying to lose weight may have the pain
    of always feeling hungry so the M&S brand "Fuller For
    Longer" was awesome – sadly, it then changed its name
    to "Balanced For You" but the principle was still the
    same – our products have satiety.

4. Gains – this is about the outcomes and benefits
    your customers are looking for or are surprised to
    receive. Some are required, e.g. basic expectation that
    a cleaning fluid will clean! Expected gains are basic
    additions such as a nice smell. Desired gains would be
    a "love to have" feature – for me that would be that
    I never had to clean again! And finally, there are the
    unexpected gains which the customer didn't expect
    but is delighted to get.

How do we find out?

There are lots of ways to find out about customers and their pains and it depends if you have a budget of nothing or several million. The easy, cheap ways are:

- Surveys – online such as Survey Monkey, via Facebook/ Twitter.
- Using existing customer data – possibly from retailers' services such as Tesco Clubcard data, Nectar, etc. but this is paid for and not cheap!
- Focus groups – you can spend anything from £2000 per group on eight people sharing their opinions on your product category, product, etc. but you can also set them up yourself. Bring together a group of your target customers in a room with a cup of tea and biscuits and talk to them – find out what their pains are and ask them what they are really looking for from your products.
- At fixture interviews or outside the store – these can be much more revealing as you can talk to customers AS THEY BUY the product which is more effective than the theoretical focus group. Of course, what it doesn't do is help you understand why your non-believers are not buying, and for this surveys and focus groups would be better.
- Social media analytics – you can learn a lot from your social media if you already have a good engagement with customers, i.e. who they are and what they love and hate about your brand.

CASE STUDY

The company – I was commercial director for Ichiban, the own-label sushi company, for over three years and we made sushi for two major UK retailers. The market was growing but the challenge was to get people to try it – the penetration of the market (a marketing technical term for how many people have tried it) was about 19% so there were plenty of people left to sell to but who were they and how could we attract more of them?

The problem – the challenge with sushi is most people think it is raw fish as opposed to the actual translation of sushi being "vinegared rice"! We knew who the key customer was demographically a 50:50 split male/female, a younger age group and more affluent. But we needed to get under the skin of the motivations for customers – why did people buy sushi or not? What job was it doing and what gain was the customer getting?

The solution – we undertook some focus groups and identified that there were actually four types of customer who ate sushi ranging from nervous eaters – the ones who think it's raw fish which they certainly don't want to eat, up to sushi lovers who know their sushi and would actually welcome the raw fish element. Using this data, we redesigned the range offering smaller trial packs, some without fish at all – sweet-chilli chicken and hoisin duck sushi became some of our bestsellers. Result – increased penetration and sales up 38% over three years.

Putting the customer at the heart of everything you do

If you understand who your consumer is and what their pains are, then you can draw a picture of them, design and target the product for them and the recipe for success is born. But it isn't always that simple – for example, there are products out there that actually cause more pain than gain and that the consumer probably didn't realise they needed!

Take, for example, Coca-Cola – a fizzy drink with artificial colours, full of sugar, that rots your teeth, overstimulates you and if you have the diet version, strips the calcium from your bones and stains your teeth. What job is it doing? Well, at the beginning, it was all about social and emotional jobs – feeling good, being part of something – "the real thing". Then as Coke realised there were a number of people they weren't reaching, they launched new varieties – Diet Coke being the most successful and others that failed such as the famous new Coke in 1985 which was withdrawn and the old recipe reinstated.

The art is finding a customer need and ensuring that your product remains congruent with the customer base – it needs to be flexible and adaptable to ensure that it resonates and so customers identify with your business and your message.

And then differentiate from the masses by creating a brand that speaks to your tribe – mass is interesting but as Tesco has found being all things to all people is hard. But Lidl and Waitrose both have a highly niche target customer base and know where they are going.

So how do you differentiate your approach so that it is sustainable? How do you interact with consumers in a way that has the right and consistent feeling and meaning in it for them to want to engage with you? That is the million-dollar question and many, many books have been written about it but the best way to go is to start asking people.

Why is knowing your customer so critical?

95% of NPD fails and these failures are very costly in terms of money and lost kudos for your branding – if you know your consumer reaction to your product you have a fair chance of a successful product. But there are also other positive reasons:

1. Identify new usage occasions – Pip & Nut did some great research on nut butters and launched sachets that could be used at the gym but they also found that people were using lots of their product and actually needed bigger volumes so they launched the mega tub.

2. Identify ways of improving products – you may find that you have a whole load of people who are buying your product for a completely different motivation than you were expecting. For example, I did some research into vegetarian products for a client and found there were actually eleven key reasons why people were buying – two examples were meat rejectors who just didn't like meat – so for them the veggie chicken nugget was not appropriate as they would have preferred a vegetable

burger. The second group were vegetarian for health reasons so deep-fried coated bean burgers weren't really accommodating them and we needed to create healthy alternatives.

3. Better targeted marketing – once you have a good understanding of your consumer, you can speak to them in their tone of voice about their concerns and problems more effectively and encourage more sales.

4. Better packaging design – my favourite example of this is the snap pots and big tubs of beans that Heinz launched a few years ago – the big tubs were great because heavy users of beans hated opening all those tins and wanted an easy access product that would sit in the fridge but low users/single people loved the snap pots which were microwaveable, ready-to-serve alternatives to tins (which are not microwaveable and need something to heat them in!). For both options, they could charge a price premium.

5. Merchandising – once you have an understanding of how your customer shops and their motivations, you will identify where your product should sit. We had a lot of debate with the retailers of frozen vegetarian meals as to whether customers wanted to shop by brand, i.e. Quorn, Linda McCartney and own label or more by product and eating occasion. Also, the ethical vegetarians certainly did not want their products anywhere near meat! M&S merchandises its veggie kebabs next to meat ones at BBQ season but then that customer decision tree is different – thinking about

veggie alternatives for the barbie rather than veggie products in general.

In summary, understanding your customer is key and from this base, you can create an awesome product range which leads us to the next chapter.

Exercise

Knowing your customer enables you to create a USP (unique selling point) for your business. If you don't know your customer, you don't know where to target your social media, where to promote, which retailers to work with or which products will work or where there are opportunities for expansion and growth. So, this exercise will enable you to draw a virtual or real picture of your customer – remember, as in the sushi example, there may be more than one!

1. Who are your buyers? Use actual data if you have it to hand, otherwise think about who the product is suitable for (especially if you are working on a completely new market or brand).
2. What are they trying to accomplish? i.e. motivation for buying the product.
3. What goals are driving behaviour? Are they doing a job or solving some pain?
4. How do they think? Are they cautious people or spontaneous? Innovators or early adopters?

5. How do they buy? Do they just run into a store and grab and go or is it a considered researched product decision?

6. Why do they make that decision so what is the buying decision tree? The decision-making tree is really important for understanding how to design your packaging and where to position the product on the shelf, especially if it is a new product. I remember when the first "breakfast biscuits" came out – the advertising needed to be clear that they would be in the cereal aisle not with the biscuits – because that was where research showed they would best sell.

7. Where do they buy? Depending on your shopper profile will depend on where your customer is going.

8. When do they buy? Timing is key for understanding customers and planning your products and merchandising once again. If your product is bought at lunchtime, it either needs to be next to the till or in the food-to-go chillers.

Take all your answers from above and create a visual of your target consumers. Even make a full-size cardboard cut-out of your target customer.

Chapter 4 Create an awesome product range

Design is not just what it looks like and feels like. Design is how it works.

Steve Jobs

One of the first things that I teach my clients is that there are no new ideas in food – the big boys spend millions and millions of pounds researching trends, designing new products and finding the next big thing. So, the art of success for a small food business is the holy grail of finding something that no one else has; better known as USP or the unique selling point.

Taking charge of your food business is all about creating wants and desires, not fulfilling needs; designing products that are so fun, inspiring, fulfilling or convenient (that doesn't sound so sexy but just as important) that they find a place on the shelves of retailers and in the tummies of customers who want to come back again and again.

So how do you find the niche and what do you fill it with? Now, you may be sitting there with a perfectly great range, thank you, and think this chapter is not for you but we can all benefit from a review of how we create the new or make the good, better.

There are seven stages to this process:

1. Find your niche
2. Create your brand
3. Create the recipe
4. Design the packaging
5. Other ways of creating USP
6. Get consumer feedback
7. Decide who's going to make it!

1. Find your niche

From Chapter 3, you should have identified your consumer and some niches – I have found that food entrepreneurs are seldom short of ideas – the challenge is how to funnel them and identify the ones that are going to work and those that need to be shelved for another time.

You should have a good idea of the consumer's pain and also some ideas about how to ease that pain or do the jobs that the consumer needs you to do.

But before you brief your chef and design the gorgeous new packaging, take a breath – what is already out there in the marketplace? As I have said previously, it doesn't matter if you are not first to market, indeed best to be the last to market because then the problems will have been ironed out!

But define your competition:

What is a competitor? It is important to work out what your competition is as it can be very broad or very narrow.

Go shopping and see who has what and what is missing. If you have an idea for a premium challenger brand, take a trip to Wholefoods – see what is out there; go to a trade exhibition such as IFE, the Speciality Fine Food show or Lunch! Always interesting to see what is trending – a couple of years ago it was coconut water, this year smoked products, including salt and water!! Don't be afraid to look in other retailers, discounters, online, etc., etc. Ocado is a great source of newness and easy to access online.

CASE STUDY

The company – I had a client who had created a brand of fruit crisps. The products were amazing combinations of dried fruits that retained the colour and flavour of the fruit and tasted amazing but she was new to the marketplace.

The problem – she wanted to position the brand as a healthy alternative to crisps but I was not sure whether this positioning would work. So we mapped out the competition in what was, and still is, a relatively new market.

The solution – we developed a competitive hierarchy as follows:

Level 1 Other fruit crisp brands
Level 2 Vegetable crisps – brand and own label
Level 3 Potato crisps and other savoury snacks
Level 4 Other snack products – e.g. chocolate, cereal
     bars, etc.

Level 5 Other products offering one of your 5-a-day
such as Bear yoyos

This then gave her useful insights to see what the competition was up to and ideas about where her brand could fit to create a point of difference.

2. Create your brand

There are many books written on this subject and I do not have the space in this small subsection of the chapter to get into too much detail and to be fair I am also not a branding expert. However, in order to take charge of your business, the brand is very important and we will look at some case studies in Chapter 5 that demonstrate how ultimately it can put you in a very strong negotiating position and ultimately give you the brand equity to sell your business for mega bucks and retire to the Bahamas – so read on!

When I am working with foodpreneurs who do not have brand yet or need to refine their thought process, we go through the following ten-step process to create the brand proposition and ultimately the brand itself:

- What's the customer pain/niche that the product is solving and who are the target customers? – i.e. what is the position in the marketplace – the brand platform?
- What's the story behind the brand that makes it great and interesting and worthy of buying? And how will that brand grow into the future? Remember Marmite?

You may be designing a brand for yeast extract but one day it may be biscuits and chocolate!

- What are the brand values – what does it stand for – what are the rules?
- What is the attitude/tone of voice it has – authoritative, fun, energetic, respectable?
- What is the absolute essence of the brand if you distilled it all down into one word or one sentence?
- Design the brand name and strapline – have an idea generation session that gives lots of potential names focusing not only on the product but on your core purpose and benefits to consumers. Try different approaches: descriptive, evocative, symbolic, wordplay, even a phrase. Be prepared for it to take time – some brand names are easy but sometimes you can get stuck. When we were thinking of a brand name for Yumie sushi, we had loads of ideas but none of them worked. Then I had the inspiration many days later of using the name of our product developer who was Japanese. It was such a relief to finally settle on a name. I am currently working with a client and we are developing the brand from scratch – she has three great names but this has come from probably thirty different ones. To settle on one plus the strapline which goes hand in hand, we are about to put them into research to see which one resonates best with customers.
- Test with your target audience – don't be tempted to ask friends and family if they are not part of your demographic as you will not get the right answer. Put a little survey

55

together on Survey Monkey or Facebook – or use Vypr (www.VYPR.it) to get great structured feedback that you can then use as part of your selling-in pitch.

- Check for trademark availability – at ipo.org.uk – and also register a website domain name you are happy with too, so you can own that space. Also Google Translate it to see if it means something inappropriate in another language. There are lots of international brands that have names which are funny in English, e.g. Fart Bar (means "lucky bar" in Polish), Sweat (Japanese rehydration drink) and Shito (Ghana pepper).

- Design the logo and brand look and feel – this really needs the input of a great and imaginative agency. You will want to brief the agency on all the key elements of the brand, i.e. target customer demographics/psychographics, reason to believe, brand proposition, etc. – I find it useful to use a brand map.

- Finally – pull it all together in a brand book – your logo, fonts, colours, everything and also how the brand is going to impact on the whole of your business.

3. Create the recipe

This is my favourite part of NPD – creating great food products that are going to wow the consumer, retailer and everyone so they keep coming back for more.

So where do you begin? It really does depend on your business – if you are Marmite then you may think at first glance you are not going to do an awful lot with the product but you may diversify so this 2x2 matrix may help.

New product, same customer	New product, New customer
New products for existing Marmite lover – e.g. Marmite crisps and Marmite/peanut butter spread	Marmite chocolate Marmite gifts – I saw a Marmite water bottle the other day!
Share the love and increase sales	Increase market penetration albeit of chocolate market
Existing product, same customer	**Existing product, new customer**
New packaging – Marmite in a squeezy tube, sachets on the go	New packaging – little sachets to enable sales through food service
Increasing usage	

Work through the following recipe checklist to ensure your recipe design is on target:

- Keep your cost price in mind – never get carried away on gold-plating something that will never sell for more than a £1!!
- Work with production and/or contract manufacturers to make sure you are creating a recipe that will work in the factory and is not too complicated. Lots of different processes add labour costs. Make it as simple as possible. Don't reinvent the wheel – get a crisp manufacturer to create the Marmite crisps; don't build a new factory!
- Be mindful of the existing ingredients that you have in

the factory – there is nothing worse that creating an awesome product and finding that the key raw material is extremely expensive, difficult to source or MOQs are so high that you have no possibility of making it.

- Work with suppliers to see if they have new developments that can deliver shortcuts to amazing products.
- Be aware of market trends but don't follow them slavishly – salted caramel, quinoa and kale can only have so much exposure!! The art of real innovation is to disrupt the market.
- Test products over life and also understand how the customer is going to use them – bagged salads may have seven days' life but once the bag is opened and the contents open in someone's fridge the quality clock is ticking!
- Ensure the recipes are researched with target consumers and even friendly retailers if that is possible – there is no point creating something you adore that never gets a rebuy because it's just too avant-garde and trendy.

Have a structured NPD process that follows both salsa/BRC guidelines but also ensures you keep a constant flow of innovation – we will look at this further in Chapter 13 evolution

4. Design the packaging

You have approximately six seconds whilst the consumer makes her choice – so your packaging has to disrupt the fixture, stand out and make your product walk off the shelf.

Sourced market manager, Ben O'Brian also says, "remember the 4m test" – if your customer cannot see the product as they walk past four metres away then it is not going to engage them so design is a massive challenge for his business. Work through the following packaging checklist, just as you did with the recipes:

- Does your packaging fit with the brand image? E.g. if your brand is very ethical, your packaging better be recyclable!!
- Fit for purpose – who has had the bag of sweets that has burst open and you have lost them all or the peelable lid that does anything but peel!
- Protects the product – when we designed the sushi bases and lids they were designed to keep each piece of sushi in top condition even ensuring that the nigiri topping stayed on top of the rice when the pack was inclined.
- Disrupts visually on shelf – maybe a unique shape but needs to be space efficient.
- Offers a new approach to an old problem e.g. the snap-pot beans, fridge-pack beans, squeezable golden syrup bottles (no more sticky tins although the tins have great point of difference on shelf and stand out).
- Helps increase shelf life – modified air can add life to chilled products but can also provide a challenge once the pack is opened, e.g. feta cheese can last six months unopened but within three days once opened it is not in prime condition.

- Makes the product the hero, e.g. skin pack on fish and meat.

5. Other ways of creating USP

But that sexy, awesome point of difference may not lie in the product recipe, packaging or new positioning that no one has thought of – it could be in something much more valuable – intellectual property – a unique way of making something that just isn't replicable or even better that you can put a patent on.

Patents and intellectual property

When I worked for Boots I was in charge of developing new products for the dental category – the key ingredients in toothpaste are antibacterial and there are very few that are approved for what is effectively food use. Well, Colgate had the patent on the best tasting, most easily used antibacterial on the market and they patented it every which way – this gave them a tremendous competitive advantage and made my life very difficult – I had to create own-label products using zinc citrate which tastes metallic and frankly is difficult to hide, however much peppermint you use.

Another client I have worked with recently has led the market in making spring rolls for over thirty years. Their USP was not a patent but an amazing way of automating how they make the spring rolls by creating the pancake on a huge heated roller and then using air to puff the pancake around the filling and to create hundreds of spring rolls per hour – most competitors make them by hand which makes them much more expensive hence the company had an amazing cost advantage and consistency of product through the inspirational way the products were made.

And finally, I have another client who makes ready-to-eat baby beetroots – they have a way of marinating them that is intellectual property and puts them in a strong position in the UK. Not only that, they have managed to monetarise it overseas to Australia – a great way of using a USP to make more revenue (and the products are pretty amazing too!).

Suffice to say if you can find the niche and fill it with something that only you can make then you have created the perfect opportunity and you should get on Dragons' Den now – once you have registered the patent and the trademark!

Unique ingredients

The other way to find an amazing niche is to find a unique ingredient that no one else has access to or you are the only one who can use it and that has only just found its way into the marketplace.

CASE STUDY

The company – once again, ichiban, the own-label sushi manufacturer!

The problem — our customer research showed that a lot of customers don't like the taste of the seaweed that is in a lot of sushi – myself included!

The solution – our development chef was trawling one

day and found this amazing fruit and vegetable-based wrap material in the US that could be used as an alternative to nori (the seaweed) which was purely fruit or vegetable based. We got hold of samples, made sushi and showed it to our customers who absolutely loved it. We signed an exclusivity agreement with the US company who were not using it in a factory environment, just sushi takeaways. So, we then began the process of scaling up into the factory. It is not an easy material to use and needs a dry environment otherwise it gets sticky and tears – sushi factories are anything but dry!! Anyway, all credit to the factory manager at the time, we managed it and launched the first wraps in the UK without nori. We won the food manufacturer SME food innovator of the year and no other manufacturer managed to use the material.

Other ideas are to take an ingredient that is very new and maybe only just classified as a food ingredient and get it made into yummy products that the customer is looking for. One example of where this has maybe been a product too soon was protein bars made with insect powder, e.g. Crowbar, which was a great selling product in the Netherlands where they have embraced eating insects but did not get traction in the UK. The research was good, she got the listings but failed to get the repurchase and sadly the product life is mothballed, if you pardon the pun – but it will be back when the time is right.

Shelf life

One of the challenges for many chilled-food manufacturers, retailers and food service alike is shelf life; maximising life, minimising waste and keeping the quality of the product safe and edible is a holy grail that I have pursued many times. A client of mine has achieved fabulous quality ready meals with twenty-nine days' life, with no additives or preservatives, just a great pasteurisation system!! It gives them a great selling point and minimises cost of waste, etc.

If you can find an innovative way of packaging your product or creating a recipe that enables a product to extend life then again you can have an amazing USP for your brand or your own-label customers.

6. Get consumer feedback

As I said earlier, over 95% of new products fail and many of these are from big companies that do the research before they launch. So maybe research isn't the solution to success but it can certainly inform you with useful insights and stories for retailer presentations. Ideally there are two or three stages of research:

1. The investigation to find out what the customer pain is (as in Chapter 3) – best to use focus groups to dig deep into the experience. Or surveys can work but need to be well designed so they don't lead the consumer. It is easy and cheap to set up Survey Monkey yourself or I have also used Mintel for more complex questionnaires. Or use your social media

    audience to find out what people hate about current products, whether yours or others.

2.   Research the concepts, brand design and logos – Vypr (vypr.it) enables you to test as many variables as you like quickly and efficiently, great for low budget quantitative research.

3.   Research the final product – twice! It is the twice bit that very few companies actually do – they get the feedback, make the tweaks and usually due to time constraints, do not put it back into research. One great way of researching the total product concept, i.e. recipe, packaging and brand design is to test the market through a pop-up store or selling in a local market. This gives you genuine feedback on what people think and whether they are putting money into buying the product. Or see if you can trial it in a single store.

There is of course a bonus with all this investment in research – not only do you get great insights into your customer and also create products that have a better probability of launching (which saves the money of failure), you also have some great stories to tell which can be useful for selling presentations or your PR/social media stories. New Covent Garden Soups did some research on what people have for lunch – they found that 80% of people have the same thing every day and the top lunch was actually a ham sandwich. The press loved it and they got loads of coverage – who doesn't love a statistic. I am not sure how much soup they sold as a result but they certainly raised the profile of the brand.

7. Who's going to make it?

Many foodpreneurs start out with a simple idea and they make it at home on the kitchen table. They then realise that they have created something far more successful and need to get bigger. They then face a massive dilemma and challenge – who's going to make it?

And you may be thinking the same – especially if you are expanding or developing new products for your existing brand. Well, it will vary depending on your business. For example, if you have some intellectual property within your recipe, unique ingredient or manufacturing method, it seems logical to find your own factory but that is going to take a considerable amount of funding.

If, on the other hand, you have a great concept and want to handle the marketing and selling but don't want the expense and hassle of running a factory, then finding a co-packer could be the answer. Innocent decided to put its energy into growing its business through marketing and selling and left the making of smoothies and subsequently veggie pots to the experts. It enabled them to have more flexibility of sourcing, packaging design and capacity with less CAPEX.

So, once you have a great product then it is time to think about what to you do with it. You may be focused on own-label manufacturing or will be a foodpreneur starting out for the first time. So, the next chapter looks at how to make a great brand and can you produce own label as well – and should you?

Exercise

This whole chapter has a lot in it to work on but it may be useful as a starter to focus on finding the niches and gaps that you may have available to you. Fill in the 2x2 matrix to identify how you might expand your product's appeal or find the gaps for your planned brand.

New product, same customer	New product, New customer
Who is your current customer? What are their pains? What could you offer in a new product that might create incremental sales?	Totally new niche for you – possibly taking the brand into new horizons as Marmite has done
Existing product, same customer	**Existing product, new customer**
How can you increase usage with your current customer though new product execution?	How can you bring new people to your product or brand? Maybe different distribution – offer into food service, sell at petrol filling stations, etc.

Chapter 5 Brand, own label or both – the balanced strategy

The value of an idea lies in the using of it.

Thomas Edison

Porter's model "Competitive Sources of Power" cites a strong brand as a real source of strength. Having a great brand gives you amazing power and financial strength and adds equity to a business, way beyond the actual sales potential. We will look in Chapter 7 at how, through effective category marketing, you can drive a whole category into growth not just create sales for your business.

However, if you are a food manufacturer and/or have created some amazing brand concepts, at some point you may be asked about producing own label for one of the supermarkets.

Own label – a viable alternative to brands?
You may find the brand is enough for your financial needs. But what if you are in a market whereby you could drive additional value by producing own-label/retailer brand? What if you have a retailer knocking on your door offering

you massive volumes to put through your factory that will cover your overheads and create more revenue to support your brand? What do you do?

Throughout my "employed" career, I worked in own label which has the image of being downtrodden, dominated by the retailers and at the risk of constantly being delisted or going bust. This can be the case for some businesses and indeed I have already mentioned one cake company that was 95% one retailer and yes, when they pulled the plug, went to one of the big boys and her business failed.

But it is not always the case and there are times when own-label manufacturing can be a very strong option. Own label represented 33% of UK food and drinks sales (Kantar World panel Feb 2017). See below the different categories split by own label % of total:

OWN LABEL BY SECTOR
Major multiples 52 w/e 30 January 2016

	VALUE		VOLUME		AVERAGE PRICE		SHARE	
	(£m)	% change	units (m)	% change	£/unit	% change	value %	units %
Milk & milk drinks	1,946.5	−6.1	2,035.7	−1.5	0.96	−4.7	61.5	67.7
Ready meals	1,808.4	−2.2	943.5	−0.4	1.92	−1.8	72.9	67.2
Soft drinks	1,282.5	−6.2	1,746.6	−4.6	0.73	−1.7	17.8	26.6
Bread & bakery	1,203.1	−2.1	1,129.2	−2.3	1.07	0.3	32.6	32.8
Cheese	1,153.9	−5.6	642.7	−3.0	1.80	−2.6	52.3	51.6
Desserts & cream	1,107.9	−4.0	1,000.2	−5.4	1.11	1.5	34.8	34.7
Canned/frozen veg	998.2	−6.0	1,118.4	−5.7	0.89	−0.3	45.1	54.3
Pasta/pizza/rice	949.8	−2.3	940.5	−0.3	1.01	−2.0	34.2	36.7
Can/frozen meat	723.2	−1.5	402.9	−4.6	1.80	3.2	41.7	41.8
Household paper	690.9	2.6	378.1	3.3	1.83	−0.7	44.6	52.4
Baking & cooking	633.9	5.9	580.9	6.1	1.09	−0.2	46.8	51.1
Snacks	630.0	−1.2	527.0	−5.4	1.20	4.5	18.4	15.9
Sauces & dips	510.2	1.1	494.8	1.9	1.03	−0.8	39.7	49.2
Biscuits	419.3	−2.7	548.8	−4.4	0.76	1.8	17.9	23.7
Jam, spread, yel fats	386.3	−7.4	354.8	−3.5	1.09	−4.1	24.5	34.9
Petfood	343.4	0.4	273.2	2.0	1.26	−1.6	19.2	26.0
Breakfast cereal	282.8	−5.9	188.4	−1.3	1.50	−4.7	20.5	26.3
Ice cream	249.1	−2.7	190.8	−2.9	1.31	0.1	25.4	32.5
Cleaning products	239.9	−2.8	262.9	0.6	0.91	−3.4	21.0	34.4
Babycare	214.7	−8.1	138.7	9.6	1.55	−16.2	33.0	52.6

 IRi Data provided by IRI, formerly named SymphonyIRI Group. Driving the transformation of the consumer packaged goods (CPG), retail, and healthcare industries, IRI provides market and shopper information, predictive analysis and the foresight that leads to action. Visit www. iriworldwide.co.uk for further information.

The largest % share of category for own label is ready meals – although now under threat from the massive growth of Charlie Bigham's. Interestingly the lowest % is soft drinks which is of course dominated by Coke and Pepsi and where there is a massive premium differential between own label and brand pricing – Charlie Bigham's offers 20% premium but Coke is double the price of own-label cola. The elements that determine whether own label is dominant in a market is as follows:

- Categories with high innovation rate with significant investment, e.g. ready meals.
- High product differentiation – e.g. haircare which is the highest level of brand in the US has a wide range of needs to be met.
- High levels of strong branding and marketing investment – Coca-Cola and Pepsi spent over £70m on advertising alone in 2016 (*Grocer*, April 2017). Low own-label categories tend to be more generically supported such as milk.
- Strong brand equity – brand manufacturers' investments in innovation and marketing have created strong brand preferences and loyalty among consumers. Shampoo is among the top three products for which consumers are willing to pay a premium in every region.
- Longer purchase cycle and heavy promotional activity – consumers purchase haircare items less frequently than some other FMCG categories (such as short-life chilled food). Since purchasing is more sporadic, the higher price tag for brands is less of a barrier.

- Fast purchase cycle, making its price more noticeable to most consumers and also reduces loyalty.

But as with challenger brands coming into the branded arena, sometimes there is an opportunity for creating a niche within a highly branded arena but with an own-label product or to use scale to dominate the market and create a point of difference through volume. So what are the key ways that own-label companies can have success?

1. Sheer scale of operation

    When I first joined the realms of the food industry, I began working for an own-label fizzy pop manufacturer Cott Beverages who were (and may well still be) the leading own-label supplier of fizzy pop in the world – supplying Walmart globally among others. They were awesome developers of cola and had a premium product to rival Coke and Pepsi. But when you are selling for 20p for a value cola vs £1.10 for a Coca-Cola bottle for inherently the same product, you can begin to see the issue and challenge. Clearly Cott don't have the investment in promotional activity that Coke will have but they still need to do their consumer research and develop awesome products. Their ability to deliver profit comes from size – from when they came to the UK, they have acquired many other bottling houses and ensured that they dominate the market. They are also a multi award-winning manufacturer receiving recognition for their category and account management excellence. Which brings me on to point 2 – category management.

2. Category management and creativity

   The businesses that succeed in own label are the ones that do all of the things that we have described so far in the book and will continue to talk about in later chapters. They know their market, consumer and category and have great marketing ideas on how to get the retailers business to grow and create competitive advantage against the other retailers. Again, this can take a lot of investment and there is always a risk with own label that you create an amazing strategy and range for a retailer and you find they love the strategy and give it to another supplier.

   I had this when working with a client – we did an awesome piece of work for a retailer – totally analysed their range, worked through who the customer was and how they could develop and grow through an awesome new range and marketing strategy. Suffice to say we did not get the business but they did use the ideas. But this can also happen with successful brands as well.

3. Unique ability to supply

   In the key criteria for creating a brand in the previous chapter, we did look at intellectual property and other uniqueness that can ensure that an own-label business can dominate a market. It is possible that this can be better delivered through a branded offer but then again sometimes that uniqueness evolves over time.

When I worked for ichiban, we had some unique elements such as the way we cooked and prepared the rice that retail customers liked – they saw the recipe as "their rice" and absolutely did not want to move that business elsewhere. We were cooking rice in 5kg pots – of which the factory had invested in over thirty to ensure consistency of rice adapting each cook time to the batch of rice depending on which field it was grown in, age of rice and country of origin. That unique knowledge gave ichiban an awesome point of difference and coupled of course with great NPD and category management ensured they kept their retail customers for many, many years and actually made a profit!

4. High barriers to entry

Some markets are very hard to get into as they have what are called high barriers to entry, i.e. it is not that easy to get started. So, for example, if you are making granola, it is possible to make it in your kitchen at home and then contract it out to someone else. However, if you have a product like Christmas puddings which are up to a year old when they are sold, it can be an interesting cash-flow challenge especially if you are making large volumes.

For this reason, Matthew Walker Christmas Puddings was a highly profitable business. They do have a brand but the business is predominantly own label. Highly profitable and dominating the market – they supplied the Christmas puddings of pretty much everyone (except M&S) including Harrods!! The beauty of their business was high barriers to entry – you only have sales for the last quarter of the year and need massive cash flow to keep the business going as you need to make the puddings up to one year in advance. Plus, they are only one of two factories in the UK who actually produce nut free and nut products – through an amazing lock-down period where the nuts are segregated away and only nut-free puddings are made. Of course, it does help that puddings are a high-ticket item and whilst they are largely fruit and nut based which are commodities that fluctuate they still make a good margin.

5. Collaborative relationships
   Chilled own-label sandwiches, salads and ready meals manufacturers are good examples of where own label has been very successful at growing collaborative relationships. These tend to be high-ticket items where there is an opportunity to create differential in the marketplace and drive the market value upwards. This means that companies are willing to dedicate a factory to just one retailer or even build one specifically on the premise that the retailer will take product from them for a contracted time period – maybe three to five years. Here, there is an opportunity to create value through working together – these situations tend to be where

a business has a large portfolio of companies such as Bakkavor or Samworths but the model can work if you have something unique that you are willing to offer just one retailer on an exclusive basis.

But... "Kellogg's don't make for anyone else"

In the last section, I have focused on businesses for whom own label is their business – they may have the odd tertiary brand or have tried to launch a brand but not had the funds and the knowledge to create it effectively. The opposite and most interesting debate is for those companies who already have their brand, who have established the market and have their own factory with spare capacity. And the retailer comes knocking wanting to do an own-label version – that maybe offers a point of difference to the brand but is basically going to be a cheaper version of what is already out there. In taking charge of your business, do you see it as an opportunity to fill the factory with capacity, to contribute to overheads and improve your buying power as it enables you to buy bigger volumes? Or are you making a deal with the Devil; giving away your points of difference, the Crown jewels? Well, you have to take charge of your business and decide whether it works or not – I have never been a fan of marginal costing, i.e. so long as it makes a contribution to overheads, an own-label product just has to cover production costs – it is a slippery slope to being a busy fool. I was at a talk not so long ago by Gem Misa, who created Cauli Rice. She has been approached by a number of retailers asking if she will do an own-label version as she has a unique process whereby she can create rice from cauliflower. Up to now she has rightly said no but at some point, the retailers' desire for own label will mean someone else will create an alternative so at that point does she own the whole category or does she plough on with maintaining her brand.

Is there money to be made? – It is generally the case that own label retail prices are lower than the brand and that there is less profit to be shared with the retailer (who may want a higher percentage than brand) and supplier. We talked earlier about the folly of marginal costing and you need to decide as a business whether it is going to be worth doing, and also to remember the on costs of working with own-label retailers such as:

- Bearing the cost of the recipe development work, nutritional analysis and stability work
- Paying for the cost of artworks
- Specific retailer audits
- Potential fines for when things go wrong
- Supply restrictions on various ingredients, e.g. fish and meat need to come from specific approved factories and this can often lead to on costs of supply
- Exclusivity – if the retailer comes up with a great new idea that would be perfect for the brand you may be restricted on whether this is exclusive to your retail partner

Like every business decision that you are involved in, this one needs to be made based on sound business strategy and financial strategy. But own label can be a very useful option to create profitable growth.

In the next chapter, we look at how you can build your retailer relationships to maximum effect whether it be for own label or brand.

Exercise

If you are a brand manufacturer and are interested in the benefits that own label has to offer, run through this checklist to decide if you believe own label would fit in your business strategy:

1. Do you have spare capacity?

   No – there is a possibility to consider a new factory or outsourcing but ideally you should focus on maximising the sales per unit and that is working on your brand.

   Yes – then what can you do with your brand to expand the sales before considering OL, e.g.
   – New product development
   – Additional retailers
   – Food service
   – Export

2. Do you have enough gaps in the market to create an own label that compliments rather than competes with your brand?

   Yes – it may be worth considering if you can create incremental sales.

   No – it is possible that own label will harm the brand by encouraging customers to trade down.

3. Does an own label already exist in the market?

   Yes – therefore you may well just be pitching for existing business which can create a tender position which drives overall cost prices down.

No – there is an argument that the own label would be better in your factory than someone else's and so you should look to assess the financial viability of adding own label to your portfolio.

But do not compromise your brand!

Chapter 6 Retail customers – friend or foe?

The key to success is to get out into the store and listen to what the associates have to say.

Sam Walton

Dealing with retailers has been the basis of my entire career – either working for them or their suppliers. I define retailers as the UK grocery trade, whether that is the major multiples, smaller chains or independents. The majority of my clients aspire to get a listing in a major multiple but there are always exceptions to the rule so we will begin by looking at the classic route to market for a foodpreneur when they first begin to design products. I do not talk about food service in this book as it is outside my scope of experience but the majority of this chapter would still be relevant in terms of creating successful relationships through which to successfully sell your food.

So, in this chapter, we will look at:

- Route to market – who are the key retailers and how do you build your distribution base

- Basis of successful retailer relationships
- What drives power in the retailer relationship
- GSCOP and how it can help

Route to market

What an interesting and difficult challenge – how to grow a business – where do you start?

When a food company first starts out, it is excited to get the first customer – the first coffee shop that takes your brownies, the first deli that puts the chutney on the shelf.

But then the company finds it has twenty stores and each of them spread over the city and they need to have deliveries first thing in the morning so each one takes longer as it is rush hour and the lovely easy-going chat you had with the owner becomes a rushed handover of product as you desperately go to the next site or you pay someone to do the distribution but they may not have your love of the product or eye for detail so they miss the opportunity to sell in an extra case, to suggest merchandising differently.

So, you decide to move to a wholesaler who for a small piece of pie – up to 30% in most cases, will add you to their catalogue and network – you are reliant on their people to make it work so you incentivise them – offer case discounts, prizes for biggest sale, etc., etc. – at your cost.

Then you decide to go to an exhibition such as Speciality Fine Food or IFE or Lunch! and the lure of the retailer raises its head. Their buyers come to your stand and if you are lucky say "sell to us", exclusively in some cases: we will take your products – provided you don't sell them to anyone else. This will give the retailer a point of difference and the food business, a simplified supply chain – two or three drop-off points and one less person in the chain taking a piece of the profit pie, i.e. no wholesaler. Well, that is the holy grail but the more likely scenario is that you decide to go after the grocery multiple opportunity and suddenly you are chasing the most elusive person in the world!! I have recently been working with a client and we have been trying to get a date with a buyer for four months – and this is with a buyer who has expressed an interest in the products!!! Top tips for you if you are doing my least favourite job of cold calling – try the following:

- Turn a cold lead into a warm one – LinkedIn is your friend especially if you use Google as the search engine as it seems more powerful to me for finding people than a LinkedIn search on its own. Identify your target retailer and find the person you are looking for – either if it's clear on LinkedIn or ring the switchboard – then find out as much as you can: do you know anyone who knows your target? What are their interests and passions? How can you begin the relationship before you start selling?
- Send an email with a short two or three-page presentation just introducing your product and defining how it will drive the category you are working in. Make sure you have been to store and maybe take a photo with your product merchandised on their shelf to show how good it would look.

- Try different angles – buyers are most used to being approached by new companies so try the product developer or technical manager who may have a problem to solve and you may be the solution!! Go and talk to your local store manager and see if you can get a local listing.
- Send samples but not just in a boring outer – make it exciting and interesting so that when the buyer receives the parcel it creates a frisson in the office. Wrap it differently, have it delivered by someone dressed as a peanut (if it is a nut butter), etc., etc. BE creative.
- Chase up the buyer with an email and then phone call – remember that Monday morning is numbers day for most retailers so wait till Tuesday or later in the afternoon. Fridays, they often go to suppliers or do store visits so pick your day – ring up to four or five times a day but only leave one message – don't turn into a stalker.
- I listened to a talk by a frozen yoghurt company who worked out who the buyer was and just stood outside Holborn until they turned up and gave them some samples – they got a listing! They had clearly stalked them on LinkedIn first to know what they looked like!!

So, who are the key retailers?

There are many different store options depending on your target customer and brand aspirations. The traditional premium challenger brand route has been to get a listing in Selfridges/Wholefoods or Sourced market and then graduate to the likes of Waitrose and Booths. Waitrose is great for hothousing new brands and will give them support but it does expect exclusivity in return which is kind of understandable – if it has given you the leg-up to grow, it is not so great to then abandon it and go off to the others!

Is exclusivity a good strategy?

When I worked at Boots, my primary goal when working with suppliers, especially if they were big brands, was to get some degree of exclusivity. The rationale was simple – if a brand is only available in my stores and there is some great coverage to create footfall, then more people come to the stores and see other products. But does that help you as the supplier? Well, sometimes – I have already mentioned how supportive Waitrose can be with its fledgling suppliers and if you are starting out it can be great to have that opportunity to work collaboratively together. Sourced in London is very clear that it won't list products that are in the major mults as it is committed to independents. This is a great way of working as it ensures that its offers keep fresh and exciting but of course if it has a massively successful brand who wants to take things to the next level then it needs to find an alternative.

It can also be a great part of your NPD strategy to actually create retailer specific options to ensure better distribution. Exclusivity can just be time based – so, for example, if you have an amazing new product idea you can offer it to your collaborative retailer for three to six months and then roll it out to the rest of the trade.

There are of course limitations to exclusivity – businesses that rely purely on one retailer are very vulnerable and it shifts the balance of power.

What drives power in the retailer relationship?

When I was working with ichiban, our sales were 90% Tesco, 10% Boots – so many people would say to me that this was not the best balance to have and we did think about how to make this less one-retailer centric. However, it did have merit as a business model especially as there were very few competitors, plus we had 40% of the sushi market by volume – so we were effectively dominant market leaders albeit with only one customer. It made us very much the collaborative partner defining the sushi market and through working so closely with them, creating our own little USP.

There are four key drivers of power in supplier/retailer relationships:

- Dominance of the retailer in the marketplace – as the buyer of vitamins for Boots in the nineties, I had a massive market share and therefore was the one place everyone wanted to come and get their products listed. It made my role very powerful and strengthened my negotiating position no end. But Solgar Vitamins who were very successful and who I really wanted in the store would not work with me as they did not want to compromise their integrity and brand image. It puts in perspective that even if you are market leader, you may not always get what you want!

- Number of suppliers in the market – clearly if there are a lot of suppliers who are good quality and well informed, then this puts the retailer in a very strong position to be most powerful to choose between them. There has been a lot of supplier consolidation over the past few years with the bigger own-label suppliers acquiring competition and thus ensuring that they have a greater dominance and removing the number of alternatives, e.g. Greencore acquisition, 2 sisters, etc. This has helped to increase their power as has marking strategic alliances with specific retailers. This informal arrangement ensures that there is more collaboration and less competition for suppliers.

- Brand equity – if you have a strong brand that totally wipes the floor with the others, e.g. Fever-Tree premium mixers, then suddenly the power begins to shift back towards the supplier. However, there have been some famous negotiations whereby retailers used their might to overcome big brands' price increases and ensured that everyone else knew they were the ones in charge. E.g. Marmite-gate.

- Barriers to entry – we talked previously about the high profitability of the Christmas pudding market being, as such, driven by Matthew Walker – this is a hard market to break into as you have the cash flow challenges of making a product a year before you actually can sell it and get paid – this is a great barrier to entry for wannabes without significant funding!

CASE STUDY

The company – S&A Foods was started by Perween Warsi making great samosas and selling them to a local Indian takeaway. She then expanded into supplying delis but really she wanted to get to the retailers and targeted supermarkets – persevering until Asda and Safeway tried her products. She got her first listing in 1987 and then grew to a business turning over £75m, selling primarily own-label products.

The problem – dependency on one retailer – in this case, Asda, who were ultimately S&A's only significant customer in an over-supplied market and one in which inflation became a significant player.

The solution (or outcome in this case) – Perween tried to expand launching brands, building an export business and generating alternative customers but sadly in 2015 the business went into administration. The key factor here was an over-supplied market. There were too many other ready-meal suppliers willing to take the business on, who were more competitive on cost – probably due to economic size.

The point of this book is to ensure that you never get into this position – the art is to keep evolving (see Chapter 13) and keep looking over your shoulder to make sure you are not in a vulnerable position. It is always important to have a plan B – this could be another retailer, food service, export or even contract manufacturing if that is an appropriate strategic route. Role play with your team what you would do if you lost "dominant number 1 customer" and have that plan B in place now so that, if the worst comes to the worst, you are ready and the whole company doesn't keel over.

GSCOP (grocery suppliers code of practice) and how it can help

There have been many bad press articles over the last five years about the dominance of the retailers and some of the bad practices they followed. Having been in this industry a long time, I have seen many of them and indeed probably delivered a few when I was a buyer at Boots, but in February 2010, the grocery suppliers code of practice was developed and suddenly retailers began to clean up their act and make sure suppliers got a fairer deal.

GSCOP is a legally binding code imposed on UK supermarkets with turnover of over £1bn and applies to the following:

- Asda
- Co-op
- Marks & Spencer
- Morrison Supermarkets
- Sainsbury's
- Tesco
- Waitrose
- Aldi

- Iceland
- Lidl

So, Boots, for example, is not part of the code and neither of course are the wholesalers. As I write this book, Tesco has made a bid for Bookers and it will be interesting to see whether GSCOP will impact on their newly formed group negotiations.

The general principles are that food, drinks and toiletries are covered, but products such as petrol, clothing and plants & flowers are not. Direct suppliers are covered by the order, but indirect suppliers are not.

All buyers must now be trained in the code – there is no requirement for suppliers to be trained but I would recommend investing in a course so that you then know how to comply and trade responsibly. One of the key requirements is to have a written supply agreement and in my experience even now that doesn't always happen so make sure you insist that you have a clear agreement from your buyer.

The code is available at www.gov.uk/government/publications/groceries-supply-code-of-practice

There are many elements that are not covered but I would really recommend if you are going to be working extensively with the retailers, then you get yourself on a training course so you know your rights – the buyers do and it is important not to violate the code yourself as a supplier e.g. suggesting retail prices and margins.

A brief summary is as follows:

1. Supply agreement – supermarkets should give you a signed copy of the supply agreement detailing what is being supplied – in the last two years of dealing with major multiples, I have not seen one for my clients – insist on it because without it you are not within the code.

2. Retrospective funding – supermarkets cannot ask you for funding once an event has happened, e.g. promotion that you did not agree to.

3. Supply chain – you must have reasonable notice for things like changing your order days, delisting lines, etc. This is one area I do find the retailers have improved on – expect twelve weeks' notice for most product delists.

4. Payment terms – again, this is an area that has improved immensely with many retailers reducing payment terms for food products which helps with cash flow.

5. Marketing costs – you cannot be forced to pay for research, marketing, additional stores and other ways retailers have thought up of taking money from suppliers. However, you can of course agree to them and they will be put into the supply agreement. But if you feel you are being coerced then you can complain to GCA.

6. Shrinkage and wastage – one of the areas that retailers are still asking for is funding for wastage. This is where the retailer needs to reduce or throw away product that has come to the end of its life. Under the code you can refuse unless you have agreed to pay it – if you have supplied short-dated stock for example.

7. Listings and positioning on shelf – retailers cannot ask you to pay for listings or positioning on shelf unless it is for a promotion or of course you agree to it.

8. Compensation for forecasting errors – sometimes the retailer will over or under-forecast and you will be asked to write-off product – if it is their error then you can ask for compensation – as with all things it needs to be a negotiation not written in stone!

9. Third party goods and services – this can take several forms, e.g. using retailer specified suppliers of raw materials, design services or packaging. Every so often, a retailer will decide that it can take cost out by buying centrally but they may receive a payment for this – this is in violation of the code.

10. Promotions – you do not need to be the main funder of a promotion. Historically retailers liked to "maintain margin" so if you reduce a price from £1.50 to £1 then there is 50p to be found. If your retailer margin is 45% then to maintain that margin, you would need to reduce your cost price by 27.5p and the retailer would find the balance, i.e. you are giving more than they are!!

So, once you have decided you want to work with a retailer and that is the point of this book, you need to understand the rules of the game – and don't be intimidated! This comes from assessing your power and position which we will do in the exercise below.

Exercise

Thinking about your current business, run through who has the greater power – you or your target retailer.

Use the list to help you assess the power quotient of your business:

- Strength of brand
- Power of your product USP
- Barriers to entry – do you have intellectual property that means you cannot be replicated or a patented ingredient?
- Number of suppliers in the marketplace – relates to the brand but if there is a plethora of brands it may be oversupplied and your power will be weak
- Strength of the retailer – are they keen to have new ideas and products or do they want to reduce their inventory?

Let's move on to building a category plan so you can create such an interest that negotiating the deal becomes child's play…

Chapter 7 Category strategy

Marketing is no longer about the stuff that you make, but about the stories you tell.

Seth Godin

I have met many food companies especially foodpreneurs and start-ups that are great at selling the benefits of their products – the key attributes, who the customer is and what the marketing is going to be. But what they miss out on is thinking where does it fit in the category? How is my product going to grow the retailer's overall category? And so, this is the basis of a category strategy – how to showcase your brand/own-label range to demonstrate how it will grow the overall category and make better use of the retailer's space and therefore be irresistible to them to list, give more space to and promote.

In this chapter, we look at how brand creation has created real value by massively jump-starting categories, e.g. Charlie Bigham's and Fever-Tree, and then how this can be turned into mega bucks for the foodpreneur by selling the business on, e.g. Innocent/Naked. We then look at the role of own label in the food industry and whether that can also enable you to make a success of your business either focusing on own label or offering a mixed portfolio of brand and own label.

Category growing brands

So how does the brand grow the whole category? Let's start with looking at how brands can drive a category forward, create brand equity and add value overall.

Charlie Bigham's is a company that I find inspiring and which achieved a very rare thing – launched a brand into the chilled convenience category – which is dominated by own label and suppliers such as Samworths and Greencore who totally own the category and would argue there is no need for a brand. Plus, it is a category that is very easy to take a concept and replicate. Indeed, I had a client a few years ago who had a great branded range of Mexican ready meals and a brilliant presentation and business rationale – she had a meeting with one of the big three and was so excited about their enthusiastic response. But she did not get the listing and six months later, the retailer launched an own-label range! So yes, she had a great idea and concept but she didn't have enough USP to avoid being imitated by retailers.

Well, not so with Charlie Bigham – he created a range of ready meals, in unique packaging (exclusive to him) at premium prices. He targeted the cash rich, time poor and actually created a marketing strategy around the fact that the products were oven-bake so encouraged customers to have a glass of wine, a bath and relax whilst their dinner was cooking. He launched them into Waitrose (where else?!). The brand created value for the ready meal category, brought in new shoppers and massive sales turnover of around £40m p.a.

And the great thing is that he hasn't spent super loads of money on advertising and promotions although he has invested in two factories – and no, Charlie Bigham's doesn't make for anyone else!

Another great example is the challenger brand Fever-Tree who came along to disrupt the market and add value and interest to the mixers category that had reached maturity and was dominated by Schweppes, one of the oldest brands in the business which celebrates its 225th anniversary in 2017. Fever-Tree has been a phenomenal success, launched as a premium label product offering a better-quality product and a point of difference to Schweppes and own label. It was helped by the growth of spirits, especially the popularity of premium gins and also more lately the massive falling out of Schweppes with Tesco which resulted in some of their products being taken off shelf and Fever-Tree picked up the slack. As a result, off-trade mixers (i.e. not in pubs) grew by 13% in 2016 vs 5% in 2015. Fever Tree grew by £18m to 24% share meaning that the brand took 92% of the growth with the remainder coming from own label. (Source IRI data 1/1/17.)

The point of category management is to take the following three elements and create profitable sales growth for all concerned – the sum of parts being greater than the individual.

- Shopper needs and desires
- Supplier competencies
- Retailers' competencies (and expectations)

There are six stages to building a category strategy:

- Market understanding – define your market and what your place is in it, i.e. what is YOUR category?
- Understanding the data you have available to you – whether that is sales, surveys, market data or loyalty data
- Gain a better insight into the customer with all the ways we talked about in Chapter 3
- Identify the opportunities and gaps for that specific retailer – whether they are in your capabilities or not
- Write your category strategy (and research whether your ideas/brand, etc. will succeed)
- Present the ideas and solutions in a proposal to the customer

Market understanding

Once you know your category, then you need to understand your position within it.

1. Define your market
   In Chapter 4, we talked about defining the competition – what market are you in? Research has shown that reducing the number of choices actually makes life easier for the customer to buy – hence one of the reasons for the success of the discounters – small inventories that are easy to shop. Retailers have cottoned on to

this and are having their own range reset programmes with considerable success. There was a famous study undertaken by Sheena Iyengar and Mark Lepper, who found that consumers were ten times more likely to purchase jam when the number of jams available was reduced from twenty-four to six and the consumers were happier with their purchase than those who had to buy from a wide choice.

The challenge we have as foodpreneurs is that we want to create the next big thing – to give the customer more choice – but this can create dissonance and the customer ends up walking away UNLESS you enable the customer to be signposted to your category within a category. Divide the category into signposted areas and you may have the solution – especially if you are bringing a new subcategory to a retailer.

CASE STUDY
The company – I worked for Boots as the buyer for vitamins for a number of years managing both the own label and branded offer.

The problem – we observed customers at the fixture who would come and look at the range, walk along the shelves, pick up products and then walk away without buying anything just like I talked about above. There were literally hundreds of products on the shelves and we needed to make it easier to shop.

The solution – remerchandising and signposting we redefined the categories into the segments that people were looking for and subsegments below those. Multivitamins moved from not just being simple multivitamins but to those aimed at women's health, certain times of life, children, etc. and then different formats – tablets, capsules, chewable, soluble – and that's just one part of the supplement display. To help signpost, we made the packaging design for the Boots brand very clear by colour and design and also used strong point of sale. I also reduced the number of brands to one or two even within massive sectors like evening primrose oil. The result gave a great sales uplift and happier customers.

2. Define your tier

There are three possible tiers that you can position yourself in based on value, i.e. Basic/Economy, Standard and Premium.

There is also another overlay which can be termed "other"!! A catchall that covers gluten free, healthy, vegan, etc.

If you take the example of a lasagne which is the most popular Italian ready meal, you will find all of the sectors are covered in the above segments – lower QUIDs on meat for the basic range, standard lasagne with higher QUID but nothing fancy, standard-plus may be "al forno" and premium will be using named meats, for example Charlie Bigham's brand. Most sectors follow this split – there are even economy champagnes, midmarket and then premier cru. You need to decide where your product sits as to whether it is a brand or own label and whether there is a gap.

3. Find the gaps that will give you profitable sales

If you have the market data available such as Kantar or Nielsen you can use these to calculate the relative size of prize of each market segment and therefore identify where the potential opportunities lie. You may identify that a particular retailer does not have a segment at all which could be a major opportunity but it may be for good reason. When we were working on sushi, we had many discussions as to whether there should be a premium option. We researched it with consumer groups and they LOVED the idea but decided that it was not appropriate as it was difficult to create a premium version of what is already an upmarket finer food product. Maybe it should have started out as "Finest" when it was launched but then it would probably have alienated those who love sushi but don't buy "Finest" – so already you are seeing the complexity of finding where the category gaps are and filling them.

Generally, you should look for the following:
• Size of the segment – or indeed are you creating a new category? I have talked about being a late follower but if you were Innocent, it led the creation of the smoothie market and owned it for a number of years.

- Is it in growth or decline? Clearly growth is good but does a declining market need stimulation and innovation to push it back into growth?
- Does the retailer under or over trade? For example, M&S hugely overtrades in ready meals so if you were going to create a new product range of ready meals then potentially they would be your first port of call apart from the fact they don't really take brands and their own label is pretty extensive. On the other hand, Iceland has hardly any chilled ready meals and so maybe there is a niche opportunity but then back to the size of the segment.

Using the data you have available

There is a fundamental simple equation that drives sales growth.

$$\text{Retailer sales } \pounds = \text{Av spend per customer} \quad x \quad \text{No. of customers}$$

So, lots of customers spending lots of money on lots of products, lots of times is the holy grail. Different categories have different drivers within them that will then help to find the sweet spot – the gap in the market where there is still an opportunity for growth to drive the category overall. So, for example in the juice market, sales are suffering due to bad publicity about sugar, etc. But then paradoxically, Plenish comes along and presents a juice brand based on detox and weight loss creating a high-end niche bringing new customers to the category driving up average weight of purchase.

CASE STUDY – SEGMENTING THE SUSHI CATEGORY

Category driver	Market status	Market opportunity	Tactics
Penetration – i.e. what % of the population buys into the category	Low	Bring more customers to the fixture by understanding why they don't buy and solve it	Develop a brand that is accessible Encourage trial through sampling
Frequency of purchase	Customers like variety at lunchtime so may only buy once a week	Encourage more purchase occasions by suggesting alternative uses, e.g. time of day, other people in family, offer new varieties to keep range fresh	Launch alternative product formats that already sell well to enable variety in the week Encourage other usage occasions such as dinner
Average price per visit	Sushi is perceived as one of the few healthy indulgence products	Offer high value products that encourage customers to trade up	Launch high quality, high value items NB. We tried including sushi in meal deal and it didn't work
Number bought per visit	Sushi has short life so multi buy is less likely to work	Identify drivers to encourage buying more – sharing packs	Create range to be bought together such as main meal/side Introduce sushi as dinner option and encourage family buy Share a sushi lunch promo
Number of stores listed	Sushi is listed in many supermarkets but suffers from high waste due to short shelf life	Review distribution strategy	Launch a range of long-life sushi perfect for convenience stores Offer smaller outer case sizes to enable stores to reduce waste. Include in meal deal

It is possible to quantify these category drivers using the various data sources such as Kantar/Nielsen or using loyalty card data, e.g. Dunn Humby. But if your budget is small, this is extremely expensive – one of my clients spends over £100k on data and whilst it is great to build your case and enable you to identify the gaps, you have to sell an awful lot of product to make that back in terms of profit.

Sometimes it is better to make educated estimates using the data you have available and a bit of common sense! I have recently been working with a client whose customer is in the Czech Republic – I know nothing about that market and have been to Prague once for my hen night over ten years ago!! But by looking at the sales data and average pricing, etc. we were able to piece together what the key levers were that would be important. For example, sales of salads fall in the summer because people grow their own so market penetration falls. So, we did some ad hoc research to find opportunities to build summer sales, e.g. by developing products that they cannot grow locally.

Visualise your customer

Part of a strong category strategy is to visualise who your customer is. There may be more than one which gives more sales growth opportunities, giving various new products and propositions that drive sales.

CASE STUDY

The company – I was working with a supplier of frozen own label vegetarian products such as burgers, nuggets, etc. we were looking to increase our sales both of existing products and also to create some new ones.

The problem – but we had no idea who the customers were other than that they were a younger age group so we undertook some consumer research to find the solution.

The solution – we identified two key sets of consumers that we termed meat rejectors and meat avoiders – they then broke down into eleven different subgroups such as not eating meat for moral/ethical grounds, thinking vegetarian was healthy and just not liking meat. Using these groups, we could then work on products and merchandising that would meet the needs of each of the consumers and yes, we did draw pictures of each one!!

Identify the gaps in retailer range

Take a look at your existing and potential target new retailer. Plot what ranges they have and where there are opportunities. You can split this in ways that suit you – so using sushi as an example, we plotted the gap analysis by usage occasion, i.e. snack, lunch and sharing options and discovered that our client had a real gap in snack sushi compared to the competition so we proposed something quite original for them. But you can also use market segments, protein type, flavour – the options are endless depending on your category.

Write your category strategy

Once you have done your analysis, identified and researched your ideas, you need to write a compelling strategy presentation to lead the retailer through the steps to have them nodding with your proposal, whether it is to launch your new brand or to give it a hundred more stores – or both! When presenting a category plan, I always recommend to clients that you don't focus on just your products but tell them about the whole category – there is nothing wrong with making recommendations for products that you don't actually make. So long as your products fit in there somewhere, it is ideal to show ideas that look at the market as a whole. This will better enable your buyer to grow his category and help you to look like an expert or "category captain". My friend

Category Strategy framework

and often colleague, Serena Hibbett of Grow Your Own Marketing (see contact details in Acknowledgements) created this great structure which we still use:

The retail customer proposal

The financial projections form part of the specific proposal that we talk about in the next chapter but always think as you build this plan about how you can grow the category – there is nothing worse than identifying a niche of organic gluten free chewing gum that will only have four buyers a week – however dedicated they are and however much they love the product!!

Once you have your products and category proposal, you are well prepared to enter the negotiation phase with a retailer.

Exercise

This chapter has a lot of detailed analysis and work to do to get you to the category plan.

Wherever you are on your journey, whether you are selling into a deli, convincing a farmers' market to have you or meeting with one of the big UK retailers, take half an hour to fill in this category plan using the following template which you can download from my website www. foodmentor.co.uk/templates.

Category Opportunity Review – One page template

Category Understanding and Your Brand's Place Within It	Target Shopper	Shopper Need States and Usage Occasions	
Market Size & Growth - *even if assumptions*	**Brand Shopper Profile** - *Who are they?*	**Category Need State**	**Your Brand Need States**
Market Strengths and Weaknesses	**Category Shopper Profile**		
Target Retailer Strengths and Weaknesses	**Retailer Shopper Profile**	**Category Occasions**	**Your Brand Occasions**
	Do they get?	**Do they get?**	

Opportunity Gaps

What Your Brand Offers to Help Drive Category Growth - *Think about gaps, think about problems your brand could resolve…. Can you think of 3 key points?*

1.
2.
3.

Viable Product / Brand Positioning

Range - *what is your range? Which SKUs fit? How many likely to be stocked?*

Standout Plan - *how will your brand jump out on shelf / in store? Packaging & SRP*

Distribution Plan - *how many stores? Which formats? Plans to increase distribution*

Price Proposition - *where do you see your brand fitting in to the retailer's pricing?*

Trial Plan - *how will you get shoppers to try your brand?*

Promotional Plan - *what is it trying to achieve? How will it help grow the category?*

Size of the Prize

Opportunity Size of Prize - *eg theoretical if got fair share of your brand*

Calculated Projection - *ie stores x ROS x avge selling price (inc waste)*

Chapter 8 Negotiation masterclass

Let us never negotiate out of fear. But let us never fear to negotiate.

John F. Kennedy

Once you have your products and category proposal, you are well prepared to enter the negotiation phase with a retailer. There are many books written on the art of negotiation and I have tried to distil them down to some simple principles:

- Understand your current retailer relationships – if you have one
- Prepare for the meeting
- How to run the meeting and negotiate the best deal
- What can go wrong and how to cope

There are a few key elements to get to grips with when working on negotiation skills.

and the type of retailer relationship

In Chapter 2, we touched on the three main types of relationship that you may come across in your dealings with retailer customers:

- Bronze – which it is very transactional, mostly based on price, tender process and likely to be one year or less
- Silver – working more closely with a retailer, building a category plan and working on other elements such as NPD, promotional and other marketing plans to build footfall. The timescale is likely to be eighteen months to three years
- Gold – where you are in a collaborative, potentially interdependent relationship based on three to five years at least – may even involve building a factory together and exclusive arrangements to ensure the supply chain is maintained

Each relationship type will need a different approach and your ambition may be to move up to gold if that fits with your strategic requirements. With a bronze customer, there may be no point investing in customer research and data, if you are merely negotiating a price to supply a product for a year. However, if you are trying to move a retailer on to being a silver level then you may need to approach it like a silver! And ditto for gold – as a brand you may not want or need to have such a close collaborative relationship choosing to be more mass market, or as an own-label supplier you may find that is the only way to grow by co-investing in factories, resources, etc.

Prepare for the meeting

"Fail to prepare, prepare to fail" is an adage taught to me by an old commercial director and coupled with "retail is detail", it is key to know your business and theirs. So, some top tips are:

- Know your customer – I have a Google Alert set up for my clients' customers – so that every morning at 7am, in comes detailed coverage of who said what yesterday in the media. This has proved invaluable over the years as it has enabled me to know what is going on with customer complaints, shares and local/national news. I also ensure I read their annual reports, and any data that my clients buy such as Nielsen or Kantar.

- Know your industry – I subscribe to Grocer magazine which is an invaluable source of information and well worth the annual subscription. They also run category reports which can give you useful information about your chosen category. I have also signed up for various newsletters such as Food Manufacturer (www.foodmanufacture.co.uk), Speciality Food (www.specialityfoodmagazine.com), Food Standards Agency (www.food.gov.uk - useful to know who is recalling) and a couple of other update newsletters.

- Know the marketplace – it's schoolboy basics but make sure you have visited a few of your retailer's stores before you go to a meeting, especially if they have any flagship stores, recent refurbs, etc. Take a day a month to go to all the retailers and see what is going on.

Speak to shop-floor workers and create a relationship with your local store manager – they are always well informed and can give you great background info.

- Know YOUR business – when I am working with a client on a detailed piece of work, I build a fact book when I start with the important facts and figures about the business – for example, sales, range, profit, market and brand share, etc., etc., business, trends… I also need to have a detailed breakdown of costs, recipes and raw material challenges.

- Know THEIR business – I always say to new NAMs or people beginning to work with the retailers that one of their jobs is to help get the buyer promoted, i.e. make them look good – to do this you need to know what their targets and KPIs are and then how you can help them achieve these through the successful growth of their category value and profitability through using your brand/own label, etc.

Not all retailer meetings are negotiations but most will have a negotiating element about them – e.g. they could be about general business updates, new product listings, joint business plans, category review or price increases.

It is critical to plan for each meeting and I have used the following proforma over the years to enable clients to look at the key elements of the meeting (see opposite).

So, let's go through the meeting planning proforma – step by step:

Planning proforma

Setting the scene					
Customer					
Meeting purpose	Our objectives	Customer objectives	Potential conflict	Why we will be successful?	
				Our power sources - what makes Fiona Claims great	Our power sources - what makes us great at THIS meeting
Roles and responsibilities					
Meeting Attendees					
Who will do what					
Roles to consider			Timekeeper, notetaker, chairman		
Prepare to take control of the meeting					
Things they may say			Our responses		

Acknowledgement: Adapted from training material from Sentinel Management Consultants (www.sentinel.com)

- *Setting the scene*

  So, you need to be clear on what is the purpose of the meeting and what the agenda is going to be.

  Work out what you are trying to achieve and then what the customer is likely to want to achieve as well. You can then identify if you are going to have some conflict areas where you may need to prepare in detail.

- *Why will we be successful?*

  This splits into two – firstly, what are your power sources, i.e. what makes the company great in general and therefore where are your areas of strength? Secondly, what makes you great at this specific meeting?

- *Roles and responsibilities*

  It is important for everyone to know their roles. Ideally you have a timekeeper, chairperson and notetaker. Clearly if you are the only person in the meeting then you get to cover all roles. But it is really great to have maybe an account manager leading the discussion and the sales director keeping an eye on the time, ensuring she moves into the conversation if it is moving off track and acting as the chair. Minutes of the meeting are so important – I always write copious notes – and write them up afterwards and ensure they are issued out within forty-eight hours to attendees.

  You also need to think about who will be there from the retailer side and what's their purpose, interests, status, and ambitions. If the meeting is the first one you have had with a buyer, look them up on LinkedIn, google them, find out as much as you can. Try always to ask people who turn up to the meeting that you don't know, what their role is and get their name – nothing worse than writing up the contact report only to find you do not have half the people's names!!

• *Prepare to take control*

Control of a meeting is an important part of a successful negotiation and that is in terms of who controls the room, agenda and the meeting flow. The buyer has also been trained in taking control and may have some fun in achieving this. There are physical elements that they may adopt such as sitting on a higher chair, sitting in a certain configuration, etc., etc. or they will keep you waiting for a long time and then the buyer will only have half an hour. Pre-empt this by always assuming the meeting will be half the time given – if you finish early then that will be a bonus as all buyers are short of time.

Being in control of the meeting, involves thinking through what the buyer may say and what your response is going to be – sometimes a question or scenario will come from left field and if this is the case then you will have so much preparation that you should be able to answer on the hoof; OR say I will come back to you – never make it up. I have seen account managers tie themselves in knots answering questions on numbers that they don't know and then unravelling later in the presentation as the made-up numbers don't stack up.

But as we know, fail to prepare, prepare to fail!!

- *Plan the time*
  Always plan for a meeting to last about half what is in the diary – so if it is an hour, pull together enough material, etc. for half. After all, everyone will think it's a bonus if you finish early! If you are doing a presentation, prepare a PowerPoint presentation as a disciplined approach to getting the job of pre-work done but don't always use it in the actual meeting – just have it there as your own little fact book. No buyer likes a sixty-minute, fifty- slide presentation telling them what they probably already know!! Think of the sequence of events that will produce the goal you are looking for out of the meeting and establish a timeplan in your own mind – make sure you get to the key important stuff which is always the last couple of slides before she is beginning to gather her stuff!!

How to run the meeting and negotiate the best deal

So, how do you plan the meeting? Most meetings have a degree of selling, i.e. describing the features and benefits of your product or proposal, and a degree of negotiation, i.e. in its simplest form – if you… then I…

1. *Selling*
   There are five key steps:
   - Understanding the customer needs – we covered this in detail in the category plan in the last chapter but you need to ensure you convert them into a

customer specific rationale as to how the retailer can perform better.

- Explain the idea – it is important to sell in the features, advantages or benefits of your idea whether that is listing your brand, expanding distribution or accepting your price increase.
- Specific proposal – you then need to make a simple and specific proposal in the form "if you do this, you will make this". It needs to be a simple one-page demonstrating the structured commercial benefits to the retailer. It needs to be done firmly without vague language. "I think we could offer you around 30% margin" – says to the buyer either you don't know your numbers OR more excitingly you have much more to give then 30%! And you really need to show the courage of your convictions – be ambitious and believe what you are saying.
- Explain the commercial benefit – once you have made the proposal you need to be able to back it up with fact, figures, analysis and projections. This gives your proposal credibility.
- Next steps and close – you can then build in what you want them to do next, agree what needs to happen to deliver the specific proposal and who is going to do what.

The whole meeting of course then needs to be documented and this sent out within forty-eight hours.

2. *Negotiation*

To enable you to make this proposal and close a deal, you will need to decide your negotiation strategy.

- Start by target setting – what is your absolute financial no deal? This is the point at which it does not make sense to trade – however strategic that retailer may be for you!! You then build in a minimum above this which is your walk-away position – this is a very powerful technique as it enables you to walk away and take a breather rather than negotiate down to the bare minimum. Then you set the "try for" position at the other end of the spectrum which is the great result and then you settle on your mid-point which is the figure at which you would be happy.

- Establish what you think your buyer is looking for – this is a difficult challenge – I often see people asking on social media what the likely margin is for a particular category. They do vary by category, product area, own label vs brand and other criteria. The best piece of advice I have seen is know your numbers and then ask the buyer!!!

The art of negotiation is to let your opponent declare first but buyers are so well trained, you will probably have to give the first figure which will be your "try for" – a fantastic result if you get it but also it sets the scene. The buyer will clearly have done their own spectrum planning and hopefully there is an overlap where an agreement can be reached.

- What is negotiable? It is not always just the price that is available for discussion – the objective is to find things that are valuable to the buyer and cheap for you!! Never give something without something in return. I have watched negotiations spiral down as the supplier has just given everything they are asked to make the sale. Some examples of elements available for negotiation are:
    - Range – is it important for you to have several of your range on the shelf rather than just one – is there a price you are prepared to pay for this?
    - Price – is the RSP flexible depending on the retailer?
    - Promotional support – there is only so much money in the deal but how keen is the retailer to have promotional funding? Many retailers are now focused on everyday low prices and so this may not be important.
    - Appearance – does the retailer want display trays to improve visibility or could you save cost and deliver in plain outers or retailer trays?
    - Location – as we know you cannot buy position on shelf but you may want to use this as a negotiating chip for something else.
    - Supply chain – can you negotiate number of depots? Will the retailer back haul for you? What % life is acceptable? Can you use larger outer cases?

> Deliver less frequently? All can be cost contributors and worth negotiating.

- Don't get distracted by time controls – imagine the double-glazing salesman who says the deal has to be closed tonight or there is no deal – don't be pressurised by this! And also have patience. I am really bad at this – wanting to get to the end asap – take your time because it will reduce the pressure and improve your negotiation.

3. *Follow up!*

   I have worked with several clients who do not write contact reports and action plans – it is poor discipline and can come back and bite you if you believe you have agreed something but not put it in writing. Sometimes these need to be very carefully written as some of the negotiation discussions may not be appropriate to note down but put in what has been discussed in the least controversial way and circulate to the buyer and attendees within forty-eight hours of the meeting. Also issue a copy to key stakeholders in your business so that they know what is going on with your customer.

Using emotions as you negotiate

We are all human and there is an adage that "people buy from people" and this is still largely true – not so easy when you are doing an Internet based tender but actually getting on that roster often involves the people element. Be mindful of this when you are negotiating. As I said earlier, making your buyer look good and achieve success should be part of your objective – so think how you may achieve that through growing the category with your brand or own label – as we have said before, it is all about growing the size of the pie not just your piece of it!

Find ways of building rapport with the buyer. Know their business inside out – visit the stores beforehand so you can offer feedback. Keep up to date with their competitors by Google Alert and getting out into stores – both theirs and the competition.

You may have seen something interesting that they can share with their bosses. Compliment them on a new launch or range, their creativity, etc. And build the relationship – these days buyers can change every six months but even so you need to support them during that time. Don't score points or knowingly leave your buyer exposed – make her look good and she will make sure your products perform well.

Be as detached and as unemotional as possible. When I worked for ichiban, we were criticised for our emotional reactions. The MD felt that this was a strength – we were emotionally involved, passionate and committed. This is especially true for foodpreneurs, but you will negotiate better when you are emotionally detached. Various techniques work such as reducing the importance of the negotiation by having a plan B, doing some breathing exercises and meditation or just walking away and taking a break.

However, the well-trained buyer has a set of techniques that may throw you off guard:

- Silence/over familiarisation

- Arbitrage – "our policy is", "our new process is" – this actually takes pressure off her and it makes it difficult to negotiate against
- Threatening wider punishment – this may be implied and not overt including reducing distribution in other areas, etc.
- Purposefully mishearing – this can put you off guard if she pretends to hear a lower margin than you are proposing – psychologically it sets a lower figure in your mind
- Time deadlines – this can put pressure on if the buyer is creating a challenging deadline which may indeed be true as they have long lead times for planning listings, etc. Just take your time, even take five minutes out of the meeting, to consult
- Split the difference – NEVER split the difference on a price, stick to your negotiating plan
- "Before you go"– just when you think you have reached a deal the buyer brings in an unacceptable demand. I had this happen where I thought I had negotiated an inflationary increase, had provided all the information asked for and we had almost shaken on it and then they wove in a whole new angle. Very frustrating and you need resilience!!
- "You are the only one" – your competitors are better… at providing information, better margins, better rate of sale, etc., etc. – this is extremely common and may be a tactic or it may be true. You don't want to be complacent but don't let these comments derail your confidence

I have had every single one of those imposed on me over the years and it was great to get the negotiation training that taught me about the way to move on from these tactics because that is what they are, just tactics. Human nature is to build a relationship and derailing it with some of the ideas above just enable them to shake the money tree and get a better deal!

Dealing with tactics

- Stay calm – take a deep breath and then try and think about whether they are telling the truth or if it's just a way of unnerving you – either way don't let them.
- Try to move on from the comment by making a joke of it or rephrase it so that the impact is reduced.
- Reframe – move on as quickly as possible so that you can get back to the hard facts – don't get drawn into emotional discussions. Reframe the conversation by saying, "let's review the financial position", etc.
- Focus on the way ahead – get them back on to the agenda and focus on the commercial benefits of the proposal rather than getting drawn into silly mud-slinging.

What to do when it goes wrong (and it may do!)

I am not great at detail or preparation and seldom write a formal meeting plan. I don't like structure or the hard graft of preparation BUT after a couple of buyer meetings where I realised I just didn't know enough, I got smart!

As we have said before, "retail is detail" and the retailer buyers are so well prepared. But sometimes we can get it wrong and these are some of the ways that I have made mistakes over the years which may help you to prevent the same!

- **The over optimistic forecast!**

  By our very nature, people in sales and account management are very positive people as are entrepreneurs selling their product to the big retailer for the first time. We see opportunity where others see challenge. We know our products will sell more than the competition – after all, that's how we got the listings or additional distribution in the first place. So, despite the downturn in the market, and the fact that the retailer may be in decline and/or category may be struggling, we think we will do just fine and grow... a lot!

  BEWARE – this may give unrealistic targets which will bring trouble as the year progresses and enable the buyer to delist or look for better terms. It can result in:

  - Over forecasting so that the factory has insufficient volumes to be efficient
  - Not enough sales per store to sell one case so there is heavy waste
  - Falling below expectations may displace your brand in favour of another

  Try to set realistic targets and then reduce them – clearly

if you are too low then there are corresponding issues but most of us are over optimistic!

- **The cost price**

    We live in a volatile, unpredictable world – who knew that diesel would suddenly cost more than petrol, that our pound would go so much further against the euro (again), that the weather would be the hottest/coldest/ wettest/windiest on record?

    And, therefore, who can guarantee that the cost price of our products will stay the same for a year? Retailers when looking at new products will usually want to agree a deal for the year (but with caveats that enable them to delist should the product fall short of expectations with no price increases).

    BEWARE – you may find yourself as I did in a previous life with a product that makes a loss for six months contractually before you can negotiate a better price. Or buyers may well want to have an open-book costing model so that they can take advantage of any commodity price movements – be aware and price accordingly. Build in some flexibility for market conditions when you agree target margins.

- **The open cheque book**

    There are two things that seem very innocent when first looked at – paying for waste and loss of profit for shortages:

- Waste – The legal beagles will tell you that retailers can no longer ask for waste support unless it is part of the business plan. My general rule is, do not agree to fund waste. I have seen waste at over 100% and especially on new fledgling products which means you are effectively paying them to take your products.

- Shortages – loss of profit for shortages is another retailer request which may seem reasonable at the beginning but if you have an order that spikes because the forecasts were wrong and then cannot fulfil it or there is a national shortage of your key ingredient, loss of profit charges can mount up especially as they are calculated on retail price not cost price and you will end up doubly worse off.

- Don't agree to limitless compensation – paying for waste can be a useful negotiation tool if you are trying to push short-dated stock into the system to avoid write off. Retailers hate waste and so may help you but ask that you pay for any that wastes – make sure you put a cap on this as it is a very expensive open cheque book

- **Costs you never saw coming**

  Most retailers have a substantial supplier manual where hidden away on page 205 are little charges that you never gave a thought to but may make the difference to a profitable business and a disaster. Since the advent of

GSCOP, there are fewer than there were but still a good few opportunities to lose money.

Here are a few that you need to remember and budget for:

– Know your retailer better – i.e. conferences such as IGD conferences which now cost £560 per person and are essential supplier briefing days.
– Supplier training (although many are now free).
– Buying loyalty card data (Nectar, Clubcard, etc.) – the GCA is currently investigating whether Dunn Humby who sell Tesco Clubcard data and are owned by Tesco are exploiting suppliers by overcharging for data. Access to their basic package of info in the UK is £60k – great for understanding the customer and your category but you need to sell a lot of food to make that back in profit.
– Invites to charity galas at £1000 per head – a valuable part of building your relationship now that hospitality is inappropriate, but very expensive.
– Sampling – this seems on the surface a great way to get your products into the hands of new customers but invariably in retailers, it is totally prohibitive on cost. For example, the samples have to be taken from stock at full retail price, you use the retailer's sampling team who are charged at very high rates and you have to cover a lot of stores.

- Awards funding – if you are an own-label supplier, entry to Q awards, Supermeat, etc. all have to be paid for by you, the supplier, even though it has the retailer's name on it – entry fees, costs of samples, etc. and then if you are shortlisted, the cost of attending is massive but all part of building the relationship.
- Audits – if you are an own-label supplier then the retailer will want to do its own due diligence audits which you will pay for – they can be very constructive and great consultancy on how to improve the factory but for a small business, they can eat away at profit margins.

The buyer's checklist

I said at the beginning of this chapter the buyer is well prepared and trained, of course, to negotiate and so have a look at a buyer's training checklist, edited from actual buyers' training manuals:

- **Planning** – know as much as possible about your supplier and their competitors and possible areas of weakness

- **Receiving proposals**
  - React negatively first – the builder's intake of breath and pursed lips!
  - Then break the proposal into small bits to enable you to break down the pieces
  - Never, ever interrupt the proposal – find out everything first

- Look for weakness in soft signals
- Use silence to put them off

- **Making proposals**
  - Open with an unbelievable figure – your "try for"
  - Be extreme and shock (NB. One retailer did this very effectively during a season of negotiation asking for extreme increases in margin and then delisting products immediately if they were not met – fortunately GSCOP has put a stop to this bully-boy tactic)
  - Use "if you… then I"
  - BE clear on the commercial benefit and how much the supplier needs you and play on salespersons vulnerability (I have had a buyer threaten to tell my boss how bad I was at negotiation!)
  - Pause – silence is very valuable!

- **Trading**
  - Never concede for no return
  - Never move first, make progressively smaller moves, fewer times
  - Test their positions
  - Accept goodwill gestures and ask for more
  - Take time and control the meeting

- **Style**
  - Maintain high aspirations
  - Control the room – where you sit

- Control the meeting – put a time limit on that may give pressure
- Never back yourself into a corner
- Challenge the supplier's restrictions

Once you know what you could be up against then you are better prepared to cope. A lot of buyers and retailers now realise that they need to work with suppliers not against them but at the end of the day it is their job to get the best deal possible for their business. As it is yours!

Exercise

Using the meeting planning template that we have talked about above (which you can print off from www.foodmentor.co.uk/templates), plan out your next meeting. It helps to do it with someone else even if it's only a friend to role play the buyer.

Think about:

1. Your sources of strength and power
2. Roles in the meeting – who will play the roles of notetaker, chairperson, etc.
3. Objectives and agenda
4. Timings
5. Negotiation targets and opportunities
6. Presentation design

Chapter 9 Managing suppliers – for better or worse

Alone we can do so little; together we can do so much.

Helen Keller

Your supplier can be your friend or enemy depending on many circumstances such as the type of relationship, who has the greatest power and whether you pay on time! The latter is very important and there are many big companies – some of which were publicly outed last year – who do not pay on time and deliberately manage their cash flow in such a way. Others, such as one of my clients, who ultimately went bust, cannot afford to pay and therefore have to juggle who shouts loudest. Also as a smaller business with a limited amount of trading, you may find you need to buy on proforma, i.e. you have no credit terms – this can drag a business under without the right level of funding especially if you are faced with buying ingredients immediately but not being paid by retailers for thirty days or more.

So, let's have a look at what determines the power of the supplier and how you can successfully make the supplier your friend and collaborator and ultimately part of your team.

The power of the supplier

The power of the supplier depends on the following:

- Number of suppliers – if there is just one supplier making your raw material then you are facing a monopoly situation and therefore your negotiating power is probably the lowest it could be, although you can always work with them to improve the cost situation. For example, adjust your business to enable your supplier to supply you more cheaply, e.g. size and frequency of deliveries, format of delivery – do you need them to pack in an alternative layout to standard, etc., etc. The exception to this, of course, would be if you are one of *their* few customers and therefore there is a balance of working towards mutual success.
- Availability of commodities – when there is a real shortage of your key raw material, then the power of the supplier will be enhanced if he has a source of what you are looking for. We pay more for something we really need. For example, when the source of prawns dried up and we HAD to get some to keep our customer in supply, we paid for a factory audit, a much higher cost price and the air freight to bring them over.
- Ease of substitution – can you find an alternative to your current supplier's offer? This may be difficult if you have a bespoke ingredient such as a sauce or

dressing that you have developed as an inherent part of your product, e.g. if you have a bacon and Heinz ketchup sandwich, you are going to struggle to offer a generic alternative if the branded part of the offer is significant. However, when you design a product, there should always be an idea of how to make it less specific – can you put "white fish" in as opposed to "line-caught, fresh never frozen, Icelandic cod"? (Not even sure you can line-catch cod but you get the idea!!)

- Retailer approval – you may find that if you are producing own label, you have to work with a specific supplier or at least a very short shortlist. This can add to the cost but then you just have to build that into your proposed selling price but again this may cause challenges around supply. I have worked with a retailer-approved supplier who also supplied the retailer with retail packs of chicken and guess what, there was a shortage of supply and who was top of the list – the retailer, of course. We ended up having to short and facing a loss of profit negotiation.

Bronze/silver/gold relationships

Just as we discussed with retailer relationships, there are three levels of relationships with suppliers:

- Bronze – when they have significant power over you and/or you are not an important part of their business, or indeed it is not important to you (e.g. buying small amounts of simple commodities such as flour –

provided you are not a baker!). This is the transactional relationship that we talked about which you may have with retailers. So, you get a price, maybe off a price list and you buy it. There may be a little negotiation over price based on volume but there is little involvement.

- Silver – this can be a very productive and useful relationship whereby you may work together to design ingredients and even products that can grow the market. The balance of power is probably more even in this case. The negotiations with the silver supplier will be more complex as there is a closer relationship and there may be more bespoke offers – but in a good, positive one, the supplier should work with you to identify how to reduce cost together and flag up when there is potential trouble down the line in terms of cost price changes, etc.

- Gold – fully integrated supply chain whereby you are mutually dependent on each other and working together for the common good – e.g. the supplier may build a factory purely for your raw material or indeed install their production facilities in your factory. Totally working together for the common good – it is less common but can be a very powerful opportunity.

Managing risk

There are a few pitfalls with managing supply which can be very complicated, potentially trip you up and impact on profitability:

- Committing to volumes – I worked with a salad

company a long time ago and we made coleslaw. Every year to ensure the supply of white cabbage (a critical ingredient!), we had to commit to buying a crop of cabbages to ensure that they got planted. Sadly, we lost a big chunk of business but we still owned a lot of baby cabbages. On that occasion, the supplier sold them to our competitor who had taken the business and so the loss was minimised but it is a consideration. When you are looking at the optimistic forecasts of your sales team (or you as the foodpreneur), there is a risk of committing to buying massive volumes and suddenly you have an over commitment on your hands – especially if the commodity has a short life. Be careful with forecasts and ensure you design products with the minimum order quantity (MOQ)/raw material life taken into account.

- Currency fluctuations – as I write this book, we are still in the grip of uncertainty about Brexit and the pound has again slipped against the dollar and euro. Many commodities are bought in their home currency or linked to them, e.g. salmon prices tend to be set in NOK i.e. Norwegian krone and you may be importing ingredients. This is a challenge when the currencies fluctuate so wildly. It is possible to work with your bank to forward buy currency to protect against short-term spikes. The major retailers do this over the future six months but it is a bit of a gamble and worth considering when you are designing products and also when you are then building your supplier strategy.

Benefits of supplier collaboration

If you can work with a supplier of raw materials, packaging and even labour then you have the opportunity of creating an ally – someone who has a vested interest in making your business successful and profitable as well as yourselves.

It enables you to have an integrated supply chain whereby you can work together to develop future plans for making the supply chain more efficient and take cost out – all the work you do on profit improvement plans internally can equally be turned outwards and work with suppliers.

There is also an opportunity to drive forward innovation together – why bring in an innovation chef if you can use one of your suppliers? Clearly you need to manage the challenges of confidentiality and exclusivity but it can be a great asset and point of difference for your business.

CASE STUDY

The problem – Sushi needs to be presented in a well ordered packaging with strong visual appearance and ability to protect the produce. The current sushi packaging was not delivering and we were approached by a forward thinking, marketing orientated packaging company - Charpak, who were the manufacturer of Hotel chocolate packaging which has similar requirements to sushi in terms of product presentation.

The solution – We worked closely with them to develop "chocolate box" packaging with each sushi being in its own space. They worked with us on the factory line to minimize the oncosts (which were fairly significant) and we successfully launched the new look which was then emulated by other sushi suppliers.

The relationship was strong and they continued to work closely with us developing new tooling to us free of charge which meant that we could develop innovative new product concepts and create amazing packaging for free saving thousands of pounds especially when some didn't launch.

A lot of ingredient suppliers will run an inspiration day to show what you can do with their products and how you can move your business forward – it is well worth investing time in and is one of the real benefits of collaboration. However, be careful that this close relationship doesn't compromise your ability to negotiate on price as has happened with a recent client of mine. They had complete loyalty to one supplier and were not getting the best cost prices and so we put it out to tender and made a significant saving.

Supplier contracts

When you are building or reviewing a contract with a new or existing supplier, make sure you consider a number of factors just as you would when looking at your retailer contract. Ensure that you have clarity on the following:

- *Price* – does this include carriage and what is the unit

of measure. We developed an awesome relationship with the US company selling us the coloured wraps I talked about earlier in the book. We agreed a price which seemed pretty reasonable not realising that it was actually going to work out three times as expensive as they were going to charge us by the kilo rather than by the reel, plus we had to pay carriage.

- *Volumes* – in printed packaging there can be very complex matrices regarding price and volumes – how much does a label cost is a very variable aspect. But it is critical to know the price by volume and also the MOQ (minimum order quantity) – especially for NPD products where you have a new ingredient and the MOQ is 1 ton and you only need a teaspoon per batch. Seems simple but I have seen it all go horribly wrong!
- *Availability* – what is the supplier liable for if there is a shortage of the raw material? Will they indemnify you against loss of profit – ditto for recalls?
- *Currency fluctuations* – if you are buying in a particular currency you will need to build that into your contract and ensure you have some acknowledgement of what happens if there are massive movements.
- *Length of contract and break clauses* – I talked earlier about having a contract with a distributor whereby we had to give six months' notice for a price increase – if you can get this built into a contract then well done!! But also, you need the reverse if the market price suddenly crashes for some reason – will the supplier be sharing that with you? What's the break clause?

• Exclusivity – when we agreed to launch the coloured wraps, we agreed a six-month exclusivity contract which enabled us to be first to market. It can be a great USP if you are the only one in the market. However, after a while you may want the supplier to expand their customer base so that this gives them increased size and therefore ability to reinvest profits in new innovation – it really depends on the product, I suppose. Clearly if you have created something bespoke, make sure you have complete exclusivity whether that is on the recipe, intellectual property, etc.

When is a contract not a contract – there are occasions and I have been through one recently, where you have a contract to supply and the supplier decides they have a better offer and are just not going to honour it. It does happen and you have to decide whether you dedicate your energy to finding a new supplier or suing the old one.

Using the power of the retailer
If you are a supplier of own label, there will probably be an occasion when your retailer offers to help you with commodity buying. This may be because they are a massive buyer of raw materials in the marketplace such as prawns or peas or through their supplier base they are able to balance utilisation, e.g. all of the cow can be used in something they make whether it is beef fillet, spaghetti bolognese or beef cat food!

I am sure there are suppliers who have had success with

this method and if you are one please write to me and let me know your success story so I can include it in the second edition. But in my years of working in own-label retail, I have not once got a result with this. Part of the reason for this, I think, is that smaller companies are sometimes more agile and able to take advantage of smaller quantities at better prices. When you are Tesco and 30% of the market, you have to buy up a lot of volume – sometimes that is to the advantage and sometimes not. Also, some companies such as Bernard Matthews have already worked hard to ensure that they are fully using the whole animal. I was fascinated by my time working at Bernard Matthews, whereby everything from the turkey beak to the feet was either used in a product or sent around the world to cultures that love each bit. Everything but the pig's squeak, as they say!

Exercise

Spend an hour looking at your key suppliers for packaging and raw materials and think about ways you can improve these relationships. Write a mini supplier strategy with the following headings:

- Key suppliers – % of business, type of relationship (bronze, silver, gold)
- Review of cost prices – when were they last negotiated, opportunities for improvement?
- Risk assess your key raw materials and their suppliers – what could go wrong and what is your plan B?
- How can you collaborate with your suppliers to reduce cost or improve innovation?
- Can your retail customers help with buying?

Section 3

Keping in charge –
ongoing evolution

Chapter 10 Organisational structure – your people are your strength

Great things are never done by one person, they are done by a team of people.

Steve Jobs

One of the first things I ask my mentoring clients is "what is your end game?" i.e. what are they looking to achieve from starting their food business – is it personal satisfaction of seeing their product on the shelf; is it being their own boss, being part of an entrepreneurial sequence of which this product is just one of many? Or is it to create a business like Innocent or Naked and to sell out to the big boys?

Innocent was started in 1999 by three friends who worked together to create the now legendary brand that sold in fifteen countries and employed 250 people across Europe. The trio sold an 18% stake for £30m in 2008 and then a further 80% in 2013 valuing the company at £320m. Now, that is a successful exit and one that most of us can only dream of.

However, one of the key areas of interest and difference surrounding Innocent was not about its products but the way the brand reached right into the company culture and organisation. "Fruit Towers" became famous for a work-hard, play-hard culture that employed individuals who didn't want to stick around. Richard Reed felt that attracting entrepreneurial people would give fresh eyes to the brand and organisation with determination to create an interesting and exciting culture where people are truly valued and encouraged to be their own person. Even to the extent of branching out into their own projects.

Its "people" page actually features "life after Innocent" case studies of people who joined, grew and then spun off into their own businesses such as Paul Brown who launched the BOL brand.

But the point is that to reach the critical mass of success and leverage power through its people, Innocent needed to create an organisation that enabled its growth to be successful and that is what we are endeavouring to do here. Imagine where you want to go and then decide on the people structure that is going to take you there.

So, in this chapter we will look at the following:

- The ideal organisation structure – what roles you need for success
- How to attract the right people and keep them
- How to create the culture for your business
- Plugging the gaps

The ideal organisational structure

The second question I often ask clients is "what do you want to do in your organisation?" and this is the one that really floors them; because we all have great strengths and traits and food business owners tend to fall into one of three groups:

1. The born leader – some people are born leaders and want to manage and orchestrate a business
2. The entrepreneur – who wants to start a business, have a helicopter view and then move on to the next great creative idea hopefully selling out at a profit
3. The doer – the person who has started the business because they love making granola or chutney or some other great family recipe and just want to make it to share with the world

But ultimately if you are going to achieve that substantial multi-million-pound food business, you will need to merge all three traits into your leadership. And start on the premise that you are going to need a structure to support the path to that bigger business. I can imagine if you are an entrepreneur who has just left the kitchen table and is selling to a few outlets, you may be thinking "I cannot afford these people" and indeed right now you may not be able to, but even thinking along the lines of the ideal structure will enable you to create the foundation of a powerful organisation which enables you to take charge of the food business you are in. If you are the foodpreneur you may take on most of these roles but they need to be done!

On the other hand, you may well be already working in a complex organisation and not have a great deal of impact on who does what. But it is really important for understanding the criticality of your role and how you interact with others to create the optimum powerful business.

So, I have outlined below the fundamental key roles for the food organisation that are needed in pretty much all companies whether large or small. Titles are not that important but what the people do certainly is.

- CEO – to drive the business vision and create a successful team and culture that will deliver the business KPIs. The leader is clearly the key orchestrator of the business and the critical role for driving the business.
- Marketing – to own the brand/category plans and ensure that the product awareness is maximised through effective marketing positioning, strategy and communication. This may also include guiding innovation, especially for own label.
- Commercial/Sales – to sell more products through maximising sales with existing customers and develop new business as appropriate and build the overall customer relationship. The commercial role is often like an orchestra conductor, leading musicians to the crescendo of happy retail customer ensuring all stakeholders are man-marked and correctly managed.
- Product development – to create a pipeline of cost-effective products that meet customer needs and liaise with the factory/contract manufacturer to ensure

products are feasible for manufacture and to ensure the company remains innovative and ready for the future.

- – In an own-label business, this role is a never-ending source of new ideas and critical for building the relationship with the retailers who are always looking for the next new idea preferably exclusive to them.
- – In a branded business, where you may not need this continuous pipeline, you may find it more efficient to bring in a chef or NPD consultant to support and develop ideas on a six-monthly basis. Also, you may have a contract manufacturer who can then convert these concepts into products and so they will do a lot of the work in this role for you.
- Manufacturing – this will depend on whether your manufacturing is done in-house or by a co-packer. But this is a lead role to ensure that your products are made to specification and supplied to customers on time and in full.
- Purchasing – this is a key driver in an organisation and buying all components for manufacture and ensuring these are to specification and supplied on time. They can be pivotal in the success of a business especially in these times of instability with Brexit, commodity price changes and unseasonal weather impacting both on availability and cost. I have worked with several start-ups who have costed their new ranges based on raw materials which are at the lowest commodity price and dependent on successful crops. Suffice to say when

the supply became tight and prices went up, they had difficulties making money or putting through price increases to their customers.

- Technical – for me, this is a critical role in the business as technical are the police of your business – they make sure that everything is so tidy in terms of factory, paperwork and design that you will always pass factory audits, have the best quality products with minimal customer complaints and avoid ever having a recall. And the great technical manager is still much more than this – driving technical strategy, building a solid relationship with the customer (especially important for own-label businesses) and generally adding tremendous value.

  If your business is outsourcing manufacture then a full-time technical person may not be required but you may need a technical input to help ensure you have complied with your due diligence responsibilities among other things or be able to use the co-packers team

- Financial control – without someone in charge of the numbers, it is impossible to get raw materials bought, invoices issued or bills and salaries paid. This role will split into the day-to-day paperwork of ensuring that monies come in and go out as needed plus the financial strategy of where the business is going, funding for CAPEX, managing currency risk and a whole lot more. Not to mention being in a financially fit state for the auditors every year.

There are literally hundreds of books written about the best ways of creating an organisation but for me there is one key element that runs through all successful food businesses that I have worked with – they all work together as a team. This can be difficult as the personality types often found in each of the eight key roles are different but as the leader of your business you need to pull these together.

How to attract the right people and keep them

Deciding on the right people is difficult and keeping them can be even tougher.

As I mentioned, Innocent used to employ entrepreneurial personalities as it wanted them to drive its business mindful that they would ultimately leave. I think this is a great approach and most companies realise that people do not now work for one organisation for life.

So, choose the type of person carefully – they need to fit in with the branding of your business but also need to be best in class of their role. There is no point recruiting a risk averse, pessimistic introvert to become your sales director but that personality type may well be perfect for a great technical manager who needs to understand and anticipate risk and find solutions. Taking on an inexperienced person that you can coach and train may be a great option and you can invest in their future or you can take an experienced individual especially if you lack that expertise in your current team. Try and be as flexible as possible – one major food company has a rule that employees must live within a thirty-mile commute of the office – the rule was put in place primarily to ensure quality of work/life balance but they also want their teams to be on site with no working from home – this has meant they have sometimes struggled to find the best people.

If you have a powerful and amazing organisation which is fun to work in and enables people to grow and enjoy their life then you will have no trouble recruiting people. Who doesn't want to work for successful, exciting companies that are evolving and making amazing food products? The type that we are creating throughout this book!!

How to create the culture for your business

The business culture should reflect the brand of your business but also focus on safety and quality as hygiene, non-negotiable factors. An obsession with food and retailing also helps as that is what our businesses are all about.

I have worked with several major own-label food companies and there the emphasis was totally on safety and quality and an obsession with food right down to the staff canteen being called the restaurant! However, I have been in a couple of less well run organisations where the factory was not obsessed with quality and that showed in the number of customer complaints, poor factory audits and ultimately loss of valuable chunks of business.

So, you have to combine your brand values with the hygiene factors and then ensure that they really work through the whole of the business in terms of behaviour, decor, structure and remuneration. I remember sitting in a meeting in the boardroom of a very large food client and on the wall were proudly displayed their values. I can honestly say I had evidence that not one of them was truly being followed. Such incongruence shows through to customers, consumers and employees alike.

Plugging the gaps

If you have limited funds, it is important to find cost-effective solutions for your organisation that ensure the roles are being fulfilled but costs are minimised. There are several options:

1. Part-time – the world of work is becoming more fluid and a lot of people such as myself prefer to work on a multi client/employer basis than in a traditional role or are happy to work part-time. This is perfect for fulfilling certain roles that may not justify a full-time employee.

2. Project by project – I mentioned above that I have used an NPD chef regularly for inspiration concepts once or twice a year – this works very well as it enables you to take an expert in food trends to look at your product range and revamp the offer and as with the interim support, provide experience and expertise from other sectors. This person can still be part of the team returning each year to input into the strategy.

3. Interim support – I worked with a client recently who had a team where most of them had been there for twenty to thirty years – some had moved with the times but some had very much settled into a rut and needed fresh eyes to see how they could move the business to

the next level. An interim MD was brought in to really challenge every level of the business and a vast amount of cost was removed and new products and customer channels were established. The beauty of interim and consultancy is that these people have experience of many different businesses and can step in on a short-term basis to step change the business.

So, finding the right people to work in the right roles all aligned towards the right KPIs/strategy is the way to take charge. The next chapter looks into how to determine those KPIs – what they are and how we can use them to best effect

Exercise

Thinking of where you are planning to take your business in three years' time, take a blank sheet of paper and think about the size of business and type of roles that you will need.

1. What roles do you have now and what will you need as you grow?
2. Which roles do you want to specifically cover yourself? Do you want to do the recruiting yourself, for example? Innocent senior management signs off every person who joins the business to ensure consistency in values and fit.
3. What could you outsource, have run part-time or where would you benefit from interim management support?
4. Fill in an organisational structure – see www.foodmentor.co.uk/templates and then work out the key roles and responsibilities for each person.

Chapter 11 KPIs and all that jazz

Setting goals is the first step in turning the invisible into the visible.

Tony Robbins

There is nothing more damning in my opinion than someone who says, "we are doing it for strategic reasons". It is not that we are launching a product because we think it can lead the category and grow market share, to add newness to the category or even add some profitable sales – it is for strategic reasons. Often this will be because our largest customer has asked us to do it and we don't like to say no and jeopardise our overall business – and this is itself may be a good enough reason but overall for most food businesses the *raison d'être* is to make money, i.e. profitable sales. There may be other esoteric reasons if you are creating a business to raise money for charity, for example, but actually the principle is still the same – you want to sell more so you have more money for the charity! Simples!

One of the challenges, especially with new businesses, is to know what the strategy of the business is and once you have that strategy, how do you keep on track – what numbers do you monitor to keep up to date with progress and ensure everyone is heading in the same direction?

> *Beware of small expenses, a small leak can sink a great ship.*
>
> Benjamin Franklin

Financial numbers are an art not a science and they are difficult sometimes to produce but we do need numbers to get the business under control. How can you manage something you cannot measure?

I want to take a moment to talk about gut instinct. I used to work with a retail buyer who was obsessed with numbers and analysis. He had us cutting numbers every which way – how did sales correlate with weather, temperature, events, service levels, etc., etc., etc. But once he had the numbers they did not enable him to turn around the growth in waste that we were experiencing or the downturn in sales. I suggested to him that some good old-fashioned gut instinct may be useful and when he was promoted into a higher job (my work was done; another buyer successfully promoted due to his work with us, among other things!), I sent him this reference from Harvard Business School: *When to Trust Your Gut* – Alden M. Hayash, Feb 2001, which discusses how gut instinct has every big a bit to play as does analysis of the numbers.

However, for the purposes of this book, whilst I do believe gut instinct and luck play a part in success, we do need to have something a little more robust to run alongside it. So, in this chapter, we look at:

- Defining what success looks like
- What is a KPI and how do you ensure everyone is aligned?
- How to profit proof your product

Defining what success looks like

To define success, it really depends what your business is and where you want to go. So here are a few ideas of success that may resonate:

1. To ensure a profitable exit – some businesses are purely focused on the end game – how much are we going to sell this on for in three to five years' time? I have worked with a couple of clients for whom this is the case in two different scenarios:
   - The venture capital investor – one recent client of mine was bought out by a venture capital business and merged with an existing holding. They want to create a pan-European food business and to hit sales of £xm with profit of £ym to then enable them to sell the business on to the highest bidder. They are therefore focused on integrating the UK business into the main parent, building systems and investing in growth. The downside of this is that the business they have bought was independent for thirty years and the people are struggling with the

change and also the knowledge that there will only be stability for three to five years – this is proving difficult in some cases for motivation.

- The foodpreneur – some foodpreneurs are building businesses to sell out and this can be a very successful option. I don't think that Innocent trio intended to sell out but it was a very profitable result and recently the makers of Naked and Trek also succeeded in selling their businesses for £60m. The secret for both these businesses was to create brand equity. Did you know that a quarter of Nike equity is from the brand name? About $23bn!!! – so even if all the factories burnt down the business would still have intrinsic value from the brand.

For both of these options, the success will be a strong business with demonstrable sales growth and profit. Indeed, a lot of companies are now valued on future value rather than multiples of current profit. So maybe the financial vision and projection is more important.

2. To create shareholder value – when I worked for Boots, our entire focus was about creating shareholder value. We had training as middle managers in what this means, understanding P&Ls and working out what were the key elements that would drive growth in the share price. There are two elements – delivering dividends which correlate with profit and movement of the share value which is driven by assessment of the future success

of the business. Sometimes this is seen as driving too short-term objectives.

3. Esoteric reasons – about a year into my joining ichiban which was at that stage owned by the Japanese giant Mitsubishi, we had a senior management team meeting and were told that the business was up for sale. They had decided that food was no longer part of their business strategy and they wanted to offload. At the time, we were not making a great deal of profit and 90% of our business was one retailer so that did not make us very appealing as an investment. However, for one person, it was very attractive and that was our landlord. He was a local business owner who let the premises to ichiban and wanted to protect his rent. But his motivation was much more esoteric than that – we employed over 250 people on a permanent basis and the same again in the peak summer season. He wanted to ensure those people's jobs were guaranteed and that the business was not absorbed into a food conglomerate and the local Suffolk economy would lose the employment. So, he now runs the business on a long-term sustainable basis – he has invested heavily into a biomass boiler and other green initiatives winning Suffolk Green Company of the Year. But his key KPI is still about making a profit to reinvest to keep the business going for the long term as his legacy to the local community.

4. For the good of employees – the most famous business

for this must be the John Lewis Partnership – all the employees are partners and therefore receive a bonus every year when the business does well. This truly engenders a different culture as everyone has a vested interested in the brand and ensures that it does well. I was very impressed by their training when my daughter got a job at Waitrose and the positive attitude she had both to the company and also how she should convey the company to others. I think that is why the customer experience is so much stronger in these stores as all employees are working for the common good – takes away the "them and us", then it's just us! So, success for them is a happy, motivated workforce building and strengthening the JLP offer and also ensuring that profit is made but again in a less cut-throat way.

So, by understanding where your business sits then the KPIs can be developed accordingly.

What is a KPI and how do you ensure everyone is aligned?

A KPI is a key performance indicator – ideally there are not too many and they are aligned with each other. Who has had the misfortune to be in a business where the KPIs are actually diametrically opposed and people work against each other instead of as a team for the common good?

They all need to feed into the overall vision of the success of the business. If you are creating a business that you want to sell that has massive brand equity you may have less focus on profit and more on investing in marketing and driving sales and customer engagement. Again, if you have an esoteric desire for sustainability you may invest in solar panels, biomass boilers and a sustainable environment – this may require some focus on gaining funding and investment than on creating an amazing brand. So, create the vision for success and then take building blocks to create the KPIs to deliver that.

Ideally, as with all targets, they need to be SMART:

S – specific, significant, stretching
M – measurable, meaningful, motivational
A – agreed upon, attainable, achievable, acceptable, action-oriented
R – realistic, relevant, reasonable, rewarding, results-oriented
T – time-based, time-bound, timely, tangible, trackable

So, what can you use as KPIs? Well, pretty much anything but let's look at a few key ones for the food business and where they may work well and where there may be challenges (see pages 168–169).

KPI	Pros	Cons
Sales turnover – how much money is coming into the business	A sales target can be great to focus the whole team on how to grow the business.	Emphasis on sales may result in a loss-making business. One major food group went purely for sales growth with their mantra of "as long as it's covering overheads" – they did not survive as sales at all costs can mean you are busy fools.
Profit	A profitable business means that there is more to reinvest.	Emphasis on making a profit may prevent a business investing in its future, e.g. in updating machinery, growing a brand through bigger marketing spend, or keeping salaries artificially low meaning staff are lost.
Profit margin % – simply divide profit by sales turnover	% margins are useful tools for seeing how a business is doing with regards to profit as it takes out the volume element.	You can't bank a margin!! It is a phrase I have heard time and time again especially when retailers have been negotiating hard. So, cash is important – no point having an 80% margin product that doesn't sell.
Volume	A volume-based strategy may be critical for a business to build and to cover the overheads – it may also enable better buying power with size of the business.	The cons are similar to focusing on building sales regardless of profit.

KPI	Pros	Cons
Cost reduction	Low cost largely drives profit so long as it is not at the expense of quality. Most evolving successful profitable companies should have a PIP (profit improvement plan).	You can take too much cost out of a product whereby the customer notices and it really doesn't work. Take the example of Toblerone and the controversy over their widening the distance between the mountain peaks.

How to profit-proof your product

I am obsessed with on growing profitable sales – that is one of the strands of my elevator pitch in my business and therefore when I work with clients, I like to delve into how they achieve that aim?

Profit is very simple on the surface – in theory, you take what you sell a product for, minus what it cost you to make it but it is imperative to ensure that the profit is as strong as it can be – let's look at how to profit-proof your product.

1. **Design it right to start with**

   At the beginning of this chapter, I referenced "for strategic reasons" and sometimes products get launched that are not high-margin items. I am really not a fan of this and try and talk any client out of having a product that makes no money – we all have the products that form the "tail" of our business but truly every product needs to stand up and be counted.

Think about some of the elements that can impact on the cost:

- Specification of raw materials – a few years ago, one of the leading fish suppliers used to make fish pies and other such products with an ingredients list that would have "fish of mixed proportions" or not even specify the species. This would enable them to put in whichever fish was cheapest at the time and thus manage raw material cost fluctuations. Even now, clients of mine may have two or three sources of an ingredient listed on the specification to enable flexibility.

- Minimum order quantities – these can be the bane of the foodpreneurs life – when you are starting up a new business or even launching a new product you will come up against the challenge of finding a supplier that is able and/or willing to sell you small amounts. You can use off the shelf, e.g. cooked chicken and marinate it yourself rather than asking a manufacturer to produce specifically to your requirements.

- What is inherent to your brand? M&S have a moniker on their fish – "always fresh, never frozen", Innocent are "never from concentrate". Pip & Nut has "absolutely no palm oil". These are inherent brand statements that add identity to your brand but will add cost so be aware of this.

- Bespoke packaging – it may enhance the brand and indeed add to your point of difference but if you can use something off the shelf and make it unique by design/labelling, it will reduce cost and also MOQ.

- Source of raw materials – when designing products, it is important to decide how much work you will do in the factory and what will be bought in. So, for example, if you are making a range of sandwiches, there are a number of levels of components – let's look at a chicken and bacon sandwich:

  - Bread
  - Mayonnaise
  - Chicken
  - Bacon
  - Salad – lettuce, tomato, cucumber.

  Do you buy each of those components in and simply have a factory that puts it all together or do you have one of the elements as the absolute hero, e.g. you make the bread as that is the hero or cook your own free-range chickens raised on the local farm. Part of this will be about the branding – your raison d'être – and partly will be to look at where you can take cost out by creating a vertical supply chain.

- Allergen free, e.g. gluten free, dairy free, etc. – all

of these claims mean that your raw materials will be more expensive than your competitors without the claims and your cost of production will go up unless your entire factory is "free from". Ensure that it is an important part of the branding before you go there!

CASE STUDY

The company – Yes, it's sushi again!

The problem – sushi is seen by most people as either being raw fish or fish plus rice which logically does not have any gluten in so, therefore, sushi should logically be gluten free. However, in many of the California rolls, we had dressings that had gluten as thickeners. And also, the soy sauce was fermented by wheat.

The solution (or further problems?) – We worked hard to move all the products to gluten free – redeveloping all the dressings and finding a new soy sauce. This gave the business a point of difference as no other major sushi manufacturer in the UK is gluten free.

However, it was a costly change – the new soy sauce added £250k a year to the production costs plus all the recipe reworks that we made with changing the dressings. It also increased the risk of potential recall.

2. **Evolve the product to remove cost**

- Challenge unnecessary packaging – Shelf-ready packaging is very much part of a retailer's requirement as it enables them to reduce the cost of putting product on the shelf and can drastically improve on shelf presence. However, for your product, it can mean massive oncost as the standard of board required for a lovely shelf tray will be much higher than a brown corrugated box. One client I worked with recently had £200k per year on cost of straight-on trays which did enhance sales as the product was much more visible on shelf but most of the stores surveyed actually took them out of the boxes – so it was an unnecessary expense and they have now been removed. I have another client for whom one retailer is adamant they are necessary and the other has said don't bother!

- Outer case sizes – this can be a conundrum for some businesses – generally, the larger the outer case size, the lower the cost. This is just simple maths and economies of scale. The unit cost of the case divided by the number of products in it will be cheaper per unit the more units it contains even if a larger outer case is slightly more expensive. You will have lower handling costs per unit for a larger outer case size and sometimes distribution costs depending on your deal. However, the challenge comes from retailers who like to have as little product on the shelf as possible to minimise investment in stock holding and also to protect waste. If you have a high-volume item this is not a problem but if you sell only one pack per store per week, an outer of twelve is going to represent twelve weeks' stock – and the retailer will want a smaller case size. The good thing is that the outer case size doesn't have to remain fixed so you can start with a smaller one and increase later. It is also possible to have different case sizes for different customers but be careful of not creating a proliferation of SKUs.

- Shelf life – I have worked on mostly short-life products in my life and when I was working with sushi which only has five days' life maximum (which actually sounds a lot when you think that in Japan they give it eight hours!), the holy grail for us was to try and get another day's life. The impact is massive in terms of enabling you to reduce the number of production runs per week, reduce the waste in store for the retailer and therefore increase your product's chances of success. But do consider life when you are designing a product – if you can add an extra day/week/month by changing packaging design, recipe design, etc, it is really worth doing.

3. **Choose the right distribution**

When I recommended to my own-label client that we launched a brand, little did I know that the key challenge for us was going to be distribution. We had a great product, great design, cost engineered to be competitive but the cost of distributing this short-life item was prohibitive and actually stopped us getting listings as we just couldn't effectively get the product to the retailer warehouses.

Many food start-ups really struggle with this challenge and it can add a lot of cost. The key things to consider will be:

- Cost of the product – if you have a premium product then distribution as a % of cost will be lower
- Who are your customers – are they local, national, international or maybe home delivery?
- What is the size of your business – can you afford or justify your own vans – will this actually create a point of difference?

There are five ways that I have worked to get around this challenge with my clients:

• Joint venture – our first distribution deal for sushi was with Ginsters – it was a relatively good fit – they wanted sushi to complete their lunchtime offer and had good links with independents, garage forecourts and student unions and we were happy to have them sell in. There was some conflict in terms of "share of stomach", i.e. there is only so much a person can eat for lunch so our sushi was competing with pasties which were cheaper and also had longer life. As the van drivers were responsible for managing their "sale or return" budget this was a bit of a challenge and after a while we lost a lot of vans due to high waste and low sales. So, when you are considering piggybacking think about:

– The fit of offer – try not to compete with "share of stomach" – better to have complementary products, e.g. bread and jam, sandwiches and drink, etc.

– The customer profiling – we found that Ginsters were aimed more at the white van man whereas sushi was a more upmarket customer leading to slightly mismatched outlets

– The type of product, i.e. can ambient and chilled sit on the same van

– Who does the selling – you need to discuss whether the distributor just distributes or whether they actually sell in as well, as Ginsters did for independents, but we needed account managers to sell to the multiples.

• Your own distribution network – some companies have their own distribution network and this works very effectively – Samworths has its own supply chain and it actually distributes other people's products on the same network. Tanpopo who is another sushi company has a very local London/ southern-based market and therefore has a few vans that take product both to local independent customers and also to Ocado. I think it works best if you have a local market to manage yourself or if you are an established larger operator who has sufficient volume to justify national distribution and fill the lorries – no one wants to ship air!

- Back hauling – the retailers offer a very effective and usually quite competitive distribution system whereby they use their empty lorries to pick up from suppliers on the way back from stores. They are then responsible for delivering product which removes some of the challenges of getting booked into stores, etc.

- Consolidators – with sushi, we did not have enough product to justify our own lorries so we used a consolidator who would collect product from our factory and others and then put a load together to fill the lorry and then distribute to the retailer – this often proves to be the most cost-effective approach for medium-sized businesses.

- DHL, Royal Mail and other postal services – if your business is high-priced food items and your business is largely online then it may be just as simple to use a courier service. I know several businesses that successfully work this way but it probably isn't scalable – I don't think Tesco would accept a parcel delivery to each store!

4. **Inflation-proof your purchasing**

We talked about the value of the purchasing team in Chapter 10 and it is important to raise the subject again here. Inflation, currency fluctuations and commodity price changes all impact on your profitability. At the time of writing, we have had some unmitigated circumstances whereby Brexit has weakened the strength of the pound making importing raw materials very expensive followed by strange weather patterns creating shortages in various markets such as salads, vegetables and nuts. Avocados have seen an unprecedented increase in demand due to popularity which has been great for sales but it takes about thirty years to grow an avocado tree so there is not an unlimited supply. As a result, the price has gone up considerably and the availability is challenged – so when you are considering launching the new mega-selling avocado variant be aware of the potential cost monster you are creating!!

5. **Protect your sales price**

There has been much in the news following Brexit of companies trying to negotiate cost price increases and really struggling to get the retailers to accept them – Marmite-gate beware!

- Start in the right place – I have worked with several start-ups who suggested they would sell at break even and then look to increase their selling price at a later date. This is just not how retailers work – you are not going to be able to get a price increase later in your product's life so make sure it is launched profitably and if you can build in some wiggle room so much the better.

- Ensure that if you are supplying private-label products you have some flexibility built into your contracts. I worked with a client who was contract packing for a customer and their contract said that the cost price needed six months' (!) notice of a price rise – well, when the price of wheat and meat went up (fairly crucial in a lasagne), it became impossible for the product to be profitable and ultimately that business folded as it just couldn't sustain the price challenges.

- Go back to Chapter 8 and review the negotiating masterclass and begin to think about how you can negotiate a better sales price.

There is probably a myriad of other things that you can do to hit that profit target but so long as you are focused on making money, that is a good start! In the next chapter, we look at what can go wrong in a food business, how to prevent it from happening and what to do when it does.

Exercise

With your team, or yourself and some friends, take each of your products and work out where are the key opportunities for profit-proofing your product. Look at the following:

1. Recipe
2. Packaging
3. How is it made – could some of the steps be automated?
4. Plot the distribution chain – where can you take cost out – from suppliers, in factory, distribution and in the retailer?
5. Selling price – can you negotiate a better selling price – is there inflation to be shared, could you adjust outer case sizes to reduce waste but increase individual cost price?

Chapter 12 The f***-up fairy and how to get her under control

Failure is simply the opportunity to begin again, this time more intelligently.

Henry Ford

The one thing that I have learnt above all else in the food industry is that stuff goes wrong – especially in the chilled-foods environment where you are dealing with daily orders and especially if the products are weather dependent. So, the way to keep on top of this is to have the most amazing systems and controls and plans B AND C because unlike M&S who say "there is no plan B", you'd better hope there is if you were supplying lettuces in the winter of 2016/7 and the crop failed due to flooding in Spain!

So, this chapter focuses on what happens when the f***-up fairy lands and the costs of these disasters. We will then look at how to get her under control and what to do to manage the aftermath if all else fails and you have a major crisis to manage.

Major causes of recalls and f*** ups

1. Contamination – there are a number of types of contamination that can occur but here are a few that can cause a recall:

   - Raw material contamination – suppliers supply goods with quality certificates but sometimes even they don't know that the product is contaminated. The supplier, who supplied the rice with the metal pieces that resulted in many rice products being recalled, didn't know it was there and actually the finished goods on our production line that picked it up. Products are tested for micro spoilage but sometimes salmonella, E. coli or listeria can arrive in products that may not be picked up for several days.

   - In factory contamination – there have again been incidents where pieces of factory equipment may have sheared off and been fragmented into tiny pieces that maybe initially the metal detector on the line will miss.

   - Spoilage – product may be temperature abused for some reason but not be picked up before it has left the factory or even through the distribution system.

   - Incorrect recipe in the products – this was the source of a public recall recently whereby a chicken curry was packed in chicken chow mein packaging resulting in a public recall on the grounds of different allergen labelling.

2. Mislabelling of dates – I have seen product in stores with the wrong dates on or the wrong year has been used by accident – this will not have been picked up by the quality teams and then is out there creating a danger to the public.

3. Shortages – I have known many issues with raw materials and packaging and it is useful to have a checklist of what can go wrong:

    *   Wasn't ordered – I know this sounds pretty obvious but sometimes the planner or you if it just your kitchen table business, forgets to order something – I have seen this happen with new product development where a brand-new ingredient is forgotten.
    *   Not ordered in time – this often happens if the planner doesn't realise the length of lead time that the supplier needs or if the demand has spiked resulting in needing product far soon than thought.
    *   Not available at manufacturer – sometimes there is a shortage of a commodity. A good example of this was the prawns that we used to put on top of the sushi blocks to make nigiri. We were running low and a container was expected from the Far East but sadly it didn't even set off as there was a real market shortage of this specification of prawn and the supplier was offered a better price and took it. This left us without prawns and a massive potential

shortage as it goes into so many products. We solved the problem by having another factory audited and approved by the retailer and prawns were flown in at huge expense to the client. On this occasion, I don't think we could have anticipated what happened and we were lucky that there was an alternative option. But it is always good to look at your key ingredients and think through what your plan B and C would be if there was suddenly a crisis – what would you do? Retailers are within their rights to request loss of profit compensation and that can be quite a hefty fine especially if you do not have the sales and have to facilitate the products coming back into stock by paying for air freight!

- Delivered out of specification – sometimes especially with fresh vegetables they do not arrive exactly to specification – so you have to make a call and decide if you are going to compromise on what you have or whether you reject the load and find alternatives. As with all of these things, preparation is the key and there should be a procedure in place to determine what is acceptable, what is not and then what the alternative is should one be necessary.

- Incorrectly printed – I have had packaging that has been printed badly, used the wrong barcode or on the wrong substrate. Once again you have to make a call as to whether this will impact on your brand or be acceptable to your own-label customer packaging. Risk assessment is key as is a good relationship with the retailer.

4.   Shortage of people – the food industry is very reliant on a flexible workforce especially if you are working on a product that is seasonal or very weather dependent. Food to go, salads, ice cream and drinks all correlate with weather and of course are reactive to events as well, e.g. Easter, Christmas, etc. To accommodate this, you may have up to 50% agency workers and these may well come from many different sources. One of my clients did actually short as the sales peaked just as the summer picking season peaked and suddenly could not get enough staff. As the products were very labour-intensive they had to prioritise on which products to produce and of course struggled to supply in full. It is a rare occurrence but I have also worked on a Brussel sprout line at Christmas when it is all hands to the deck as there were not enough staff to get everything packed in time for the Christmas sprout order.

Clearly labour flexibility keeps costs down but a strong back-up crew of people, albeit agency, should help to alleviate some of the problems. Also, planning helps – one retailer was planning a last-minute change to a New Year's Day launch which would have meant we needed the full contingent of staff, however, many had been signed off for holidays as normally they would not be needed. The launch date was negotiated to later in the year and the problem was averted!

5. Loss of power – When I worked with ichiban, they were based in the countryside and we had two major power outages. On one occasion a combine harvester accidentally drove into a power line causing a fire – fortunately the farmer was fine but we lost power and unfortunately an afternoon's production. Prior to this there had been an electricity cable cut through when the road was being dug up and again we lost power.

    The solution – to invest in a generator!! This took some commissioning and working through but now the back-up plan is in place and hopefully there will be no further issues.

6. Substandard products – Product quality is one of the key elements that needs to be on point every day, every week throughout the year. It is not acceptable to over or under deliver on product specification for three reasons:

    *   Legality – a product needs to comply with its specification, nutritional and ingredients declarations, especially if the % of the QUID products are not correct.
    *   Safety – the product may not be safe to eat if it is not produced in the correct way.
    *   Organoleptics – if your product does not comply with your quality standards then it may taste, look or smell different to normal. The customer may actually prefer your non-compliant product and

then be disappointed that it has changed. Either way, brand or own label, you need consistency, of course, and when you are below those standards, you have to have a risk assessment process that enables you to make a decision whether to let the product go into the marketplace – and of course, only if it is safe and legal to do so.

7. Mislabelling of products – One of the most common sources of recall at the moment is allergen recalls where the product may contain one of the key allergens. The problem may arise that your product does not obviously contain one of these but the individual ingredients may also have allergens in their recipe that do not show up or your supplier may not have flagged them to you. Always include in your risk analysis when designing new products or using new suppliers what allergens are in there. Last year ten people died from allergen-related deaths with the allergen being in the food – a sobering thought.

8. Miscommunication of promotions/pricing, etc. – Incorrect pricing and promotional stickering can trigger recalls although fortunately not public ones as they do not result in issues for customer safety. I have had several issues whereby products have not been set up correctly in store – pitfalls to watch out for include:

- Retailers' differential pricing – some of the

retailers add on a % for their convenience stores – this can be done automatically unless a product is set up as price marked. It will then scan at a different price to that on the product and of course that is illegal – although if it is scanning at less than the price on the pack then that is legal but still not acceptable.

- Promotional stickers – if you have put a sticker on a promotion, you have to be absolutely certain that the product will have sold through once the product comes off deal. I am not keen on stickering promotions for this very reason – fortunately with something like sushi only having a five-day life you can sell it through very quickly but even so it is a source of recalls and needs to have a system in place to avoid it.

9. Safety and staff welfare – It goes without saying that safety and staff welfare are paramount in any business. Equipment needs to be safe and fit for purpose and staff need to be trained in all aspects of keeping both themselves and the foods they provide safe. There have been many examples of where food companies have been found wanting and fined for non-compliance with safety procedures leading to injury or even death to their staff. This of course is unacceptable for the staff but also has an impact on company reputation and can impact on brand standards, etc.

CASE STUDY

The company – Genius are the leading gluten-free bread brand in the UK and were making both their own brand and also retailer brands.

The problem – in 2015, they had what the Grocer called "the recall of the year". Twenty-four of their products, both brand and the own label, were recalled due to contamination with a dry ingredient that should not have been in the production hall.

The solution – the recall was handled in textbook fashion with the CEO, Roz Cushieri, communicating effectively with customers and consumers alike. And the brand bounced back and is still in growth turning over £47m and up 13% year on year.

Cost of disasters and mistakes

The cost of mistakes, recalls and the like can cost thousands and sometimes millions of pounds in lost revenue – sometimes the brand never recovers.

The metal contamination that I referred to earlier, cost nearly £500k when you took into account lost sales, loss of profit compensation and the write-off of contaminated stock. The insurance covered some of the losses but definitely not the loss of profit which the client tried to claim from the supplier – negotiations were ongoing a year later!!

Some of the costs that may be involved include:

- Wasted product stock
- Wasted raw materials
- Charges by retailers – loss of profit, wasted stock
- Loss of customer loyalty – damage to brand equity
- Fines and prosecution for negligence
- Compensation to affected customer

And in the worst-case scenario, there is personal prosecution for the teams involved and potentially criminal records and even prison – a man was prosecuted in Teesside and given three months' custodial sentence for poor hygiene and other issues and another case had a business fined £71k.

There are unfortunately people other than the f***-up fairy who are out to challenge our business and in 2016, threat assessment critical control points or TACCP was included as part of the BRC audit.

The purpose of undertaking a TACCP assessment is to address the fundamental issues surrounding:

- Deliberate contamination of food or packaging materials.
- Food fraud – This may involve the sale of meat from animals that have been stolen and/or illegally slaughtered, as well as wild game animals like deer that may have been poached.

CASE STUDY

The problem – In 2013, a number of suppliers of minced beef supplied horse instead of beef. This found its way into a number of lasagnes and other Italian ready meals under Findus and Tesco brand resulting in recalls and public outcry.

The outcome – the impact was far reaching not just on the ready meal market but supermarkets over all.

Consumer trust in supermarkets fell from 69% pre horse-gate to 35% post (Source One Poll survey, Feb 2013).

Market share of various categories fell – e.g. Frozen ready meals –13% and chilled ready meals –3%. £300m was wiped off Tesco shares. Not to mention eighteen million ready meals that were thrown away.

Four years on, the market has recovered but it continues to be a challenge for the industry and only recently we had a recurrence in Brazil but this time the UK market was more secure and it has not found its way into the food chain.

• Authenticity – products can be substituted with a cheaper alternative, for example, farmed salmon sold as wild, and basmati rice adulterated with cheaper varieties. Or there can be false statements about the source of ingredients, i.e. their geographic, plant or animal origin. When I was working with Tesco on own-label products, they would only allow two sources of tuna as they had risk assessed other sources but could not guarantee that it had been line caught which is their policy now for all tuna. Recently turkey was sold as halal lamb resulting in a £45k fine.

• Vulnerability – it is important to conduct a risk assessment to identify the raw materials that you may have in your products to then manage their risk of contamination.

Ensure you protect your business by installing a TACCP process to ensure you have a regular process in place whereby you do regular daily horizon scanning to see if anyone else is having any issues with ingredients, raw materials, etc. and if there is a trend forming that you need to be aware of and protect your business from. More information on www.food.gov.uk.

Responsibilities of due diligence
The legal definition of due diligence is fairly broad – reasonable steps taken by a person to avoid committing a tort or offence.

Customer expectations, i.e. retailer – the retailer and your ultimate customer is relying on you to do your due diligence and ensure that your suppliers are audited and safe. If you are supplying own label you will find that there is a very short list of suppliers that you can use for meat, fish, poultry and other commodities whereby the retailer wants to protect their integrity but you still have the responsibility of due diligence and whilst it is not possible to visit all suppliers please make sure you have followed the BRC procedures.

So how do you manage to keep ahead of the game and ensure that the f***-up fairy doesn't visit too many times?

- Good systems – the whole point of BRC and the other factory standards is to ensure that you produce consistently good quality legal products. If you have good systems, e.g. ERP, quality monitoring and product design software, then you are more likely to ensure that most of the challenges are managed out systematically.
- Risk analysis – I like to work with my clients and ask a lot of the time what can go wrong? I am by nature an optimist and for these pieces of work you really need a balance in the team (as is always the case!!) so that you can have someone who really can think through all the problems that will come along and then the optimists will come up with the solutions.
- Contingency planning – sometimes it just isn't possible to have a contingency or it will be a worst-case scenario. No one foresaw the floods in Spain coming in 2017 which left £5m wiped off the lettuce market as there were just not enough lettuces in the system. The retailers did have a contingency of bringing product over from the US but at a significant cost. But as I mentioned above – for your key ingredients, you need to think through a plan B for when you cannot source the raw materials.

- People management – there are several ways that you can better enable your people to prevent problems and disasters:

    - Balance of staff – if you have a manufacturing staff that has a split between agency and permanent staff then challenges can arise whereby the agency staff may not be as steeped in the culture of quality as your permanent employees. Keeping agency to a minimum ensures consistency, reduces the amount of training required and generally improves quality but may be more costly and less flexible.
    - Culture of quality – if everyone is obsessed with quality from ensuring that the staff toilets are clean to the update of social media, then it is more likely you will have staff that will be proud of their products and ensure that nothing goes out of the door that they are not proud of and knows adheres to the specification requirements.
    - Training – it is a critical part of the BRC requirement that staff are trained appropriately and this forms part of the culture for quality and consistency.

- Keeping ahead of legislation – BRC, Salsa, retailer-own audit standards – it is critical to ensure that your business is aware of legislation and that when it changes, you are updated. But it's not just the audit requirements – networking can be a tremendous help in preventing problems – talking to suppliers, retailers and

even competitors can keep you ahead of what is go.
on in the industry and what may be coming down the
line in terms of challenges and problems.

Crisis management

So, what do you do if it does go wrong and you have a crisis
(and it is likely that you will at some point)? I have managed
several food issues, such as recalls, in my life on both sides
of the desk, as a buyer and a supplier.

I have an image of Lance Corporal Jones in Dad's Army
"Don't panic, don't panic!" scenario. But this is good advice
– you should not need to panic if you have been following
your systems, setting up your contingency plans and know
what to do if the emergency occurs.

The key to successful management of a crisis is
communication. For some reason recalls always seem to
happen on a Friday afternoon or late in the evening or
when key people are missing – I have no idea if this is true
statistically but my last recall, when we discovered the metal
contamination in our sushi rice, was certainly when our
MD was on holiday. The whole process was a masterclass
in how to manage a difficult situation. The customer was
informed, alternative rice identified, factory visited by
customer next day and within twenty-four hours we were
back in production. We were also commended for being the
ones who identified the problem and were able to flag it
up and eliminate any risk of consumer harm. But the cost
to the business was considerable – we were charged loss
of profit compensation by all our customers and of course

It is possible to insure against the problems and of course most companies do take out insurance that extends beyond the third-party indemnity. I did review insurance for a client and we tried to insure against the retailer claiming loss of profit but not surprisingly that was not possible as it is potentially a considerable sum of money. But you can insure for your own losses in the case of crisis so long as you can prove that there has not been any negligence – hence the need for rigorous systems!

To conclude, I have tried to focus on challenges that come along that can be prevented by good systems and effective management. There are always going to be things you didn't see coming but if you manage at least 95% of them successfully then you have the energy to deal with the truly unexpected f*** ups!

Exercise

Have a look at the TACCP requirements and think how you can install the process in your business – Campden BRI have a great explanatory video – https://www.campdenbri.co.uk/webinars/threat-assessment-critical-control-point.php

Chapter 13 Evolution not revolution

Even if you are on the right track, you will eventually get run over if you stay there.

Will Rogers

Keeping up with the ever-changing world is a challenge but one that every food business needs to keep on top of to ensure that they are not overtaken by up and coming disruptive businesses.

Evolution can go full circle – let's take the example of food retailing. The world of food retailing started with local food markets where people would bring their locally made/grown products to sell. This then evolved into small local shops, again more than likely selling local produce but then bringing in a few factory-manufactured goods. The retail chains then grew and developed into the ones we know today – Sainsbury's, Tesco, Asda – starting with supermarkets and then creating massive hypermarkets. Our shopping habits became big shops once a week with maybe the odd top-up shop at the local independent corner shop.

The retailers then recognised the opportunity and created their own corner shops such as Sainsbury's Local and Tesco Express. And then finally farmers' markets and local weekend food markets became popular and pop-up shops have become fashionable bringing us back full circle – the circle of retail life!

But there are other interesting paradoxes whereby the market is changing and being disrupted. One such area is distribution – Graze is a good example of how an awesome idea of online snacks delivered to your door has now became a retail snack offered in most of the main retailers. The brand was about having healthy snacks delivered and yet that branding has stuck and proved transferable to the world of retail. The results for the Graze company are £70m with sales growth of 29% although the sales growth has slowed as they have moved into the retail arena but profit has dropped to £7.6m from £9.5m – costs of investing in retailers? Similarly, Hello Fresh has gained a traditional retailer distribution with Sainsbury's after being a purely online distributor.

Graze has also benefited from a second phenomenon of the removal of confectionery from the tills – people still want to be buy snacks and Graze, Trek, Bounce and others are benefiting from this growth of "healthy alternatives" to a Mars Bar. I have no idea if Mars sales have suffered but it is likely that their impulse sales are definitely down – I noticed that Mars has launched a protein Mars Bar – I thought the regular one helped you work, rest and play, but anyway!!

So, how do we keep ahead of the curve and make sure that we evolve to keep up with the changing world but still keep the essence of our brand and food business? There is a great book call *The E Myth* by Michael Gerber who talks about how innovation can be one tiny thing – changing how you talk to customers coming into a store can increase sales by 10%, just by how you say hello! Or by the clothes you wear. This is probably contrary to most people's concept of innovation which is doing something major such as creating a new product or entirely changing a factory process.

So, how do you keep ensuring that your product range keeps fresh and ahead of the competition and generates the ideas that give you that one tiny, game-changing step forward and if it is more significant – how do you fund it?

The innovation process

Paradoxically, although routine is the enemy of creativity, you do need a structure in which your creative ideas can grow such as:

1. Innovation champion – it is helpful to have a head of innovation who owns innovation through the business, possibly in marketing or new product development who will help drive ideas through. The challenge I have seen with many clients is that they happily have a set of innovation projects but the day-to-day pressures mean that it doesn't get the absolute priority it deserves.
2. Innovation KPIs – this may be part of a pr

improvement programme for more general innovation and then for products/marketing, etc. this could be more specific. It is important to get the team aligned and engender a culture of evolution and change for all, otherwise the poor innovation champion will be pushing water uphill!

3. Innovation management – it is good to hold regular monthly meetings that only focus on innovation ideas and review how you can be disruptive in the market. And once or twice a year, get off site and spend some time using the techniques below to generate some great ideas:

Building a creative culture

Routine is the enemy of creativity yet the friend of a well-run quality-based factory. If you have the well-run systems that I wrote about to help prevent the f***-up fairy, then you will want your teams on the shop floor to follow the rules. But you need to balance this regularity with a more fluid approach to creativity.

You need to engender a creative culture that can comfortably sit alongside your day-to-day structure. Some ideas include:

centive scheme – I have worked with
:s who encouraged suggestions for
ovement through an incentive scheme
lea generator would receive a percentage

of the profits gained from their idea. They would be formally reviewed and feedback given on a monthly basis through the staff association meeting.

2. Team rotation – sometimes bringing fresh eyes to each job role can really help to give a fresh perspective. When I am asked to work with a client on taking cost out of a business, I ask to arrange a factory walk-around by non-factory personnel like myself who often ask daft questions about why the factory does things in certain ways. This can often challenge assumptions and norms and create opportunities to reduce cost.

3. Off-site creativity days – I like to take a team off site so that they can totally focus on their new ideas and how to take the business forward. There are some great ways of doing this and I have run many idea generation sessions like this.

4. No-blame risk taking – this is a bit of a challenge – we are trained from an early age to assess ideas and find problems in them. Clearly if you are working in a food factory, you do not want to take risks with safety or quality but it may be worth being more entrepreneurial and enabling teams to be more risk taking.

5. Creative play – some businesses like to see their people "working" – head down at the desk. But actually, my best ideas come to me in the shower, when I am out

shopping or at three in the morning when I can't sleep. I encourage NPD, commercial and marketing to get out as much as possible to different places for ideas – you can do a fairly standard review of stores in London visiting Source, Harrods food hall, Selfridges, Wholefoods, M&S Marble Arch and Borough Market. This will give you a great overview of food trends but go to Liberty and Paperchase and look at designs, try a gift show or art exhibition or just walk down the street and look in shop windows.

In the office as well, it is great to have a play area where you can take time out from the computer – read magazines, doodle, and generally let the creative mind run free. Clearly you need to make sure that this area does not become the sole focus of your team but there needs to be a percentage of time devoted to this – maybe 10% of time. People will be more efficient in the rest of their jobs as well!

6. Use of consultants and interims – not wanting to promote myself, BUT, one way of bringing fresh eyes is to bring in consultants with a wide range of experience in the food industry who will be able to look at your business with a different perspective. I have used several chefs and NPD interims to come in and work on a specific project such as identifying new recipes – they only do a couple of weeks' work but you then get a bank of awesome ideas to roll out over the next year. Ichiban brought in an interim factory manager as maternity cover and he didn't just do

the job but gave a lot of new ideas to the business for improving waste, reducing labour costs and increasing profitability. A good investment all round!

7. Changes in legislation – I mentioned the removal of confectionery from tills creating the growth of Bounce, Trek, etc. but it is good to review all food legislation changes and brainstorm what implications they may have. Indeed, putting mini chillers at the tills would be good to offer mini chilled snacks such as mini salads, sushi, etc. It would require investment from retailers but could have a future!

Generating ideas to keep your business ahead of the game

Every so often, maybe once a month, take time out to review your offer and position in the marketplace to enable idea generation for innovative solutions. Focus on one or more of the following elements at each session:

*   product concepts
*   new distribution channels
*   manufacturing methods
*   product quality
*   costs of goods – supply
*   people and organisation

Or focus on a specific problem that is holding you back and use an idea generation technique such as one of these:

1. **SWOT analysis**

   This is a great way of getting everyone individually to critique the business. This can then be consolidated and everyone can share ideas. Here's an example of one I did for a client of mine who made vegetarian products:

Strengths	Weaknesses
• Profitable business • Well-invested factory • Excellent audit scores, e.g. PIU, BRC, etc. • Strong NPD team • Good buying power from European ownership	• Retail business under performing on profit • Lack of consumer insights and understanding • Lack of true innovation • Lack of use of protein alternatives such as soya, etc.
Opportunities	**Threats**
• Invest in consumer research • Redevelop products to take out cost • Diversify into other markets • Build brand for food service • Innovate into new ideas using current factory and partners	• Retailer tender processes • Competition from US from vegetarian and vegan products • Strength of brands such as Quorn and Linda McCartney • Competition from chilled

   We then took each of the opportunities and built a strategy plan, generating innovation streams for new products and positioning.

2. **Idea generation technique**

   Sometimes we need to think more laterally about our products especially if we are totally immersed in the business.

A fun way to do this is to think about something totally unrelated such as an umbrella and think of all the great reasons why that works as a product and also its failings.

E.g. Good points:

- Keeps the rain off
- Can be used as a sunshade as well
- Can have a pretty design
- Can be used as a walking stick
- Can be used as a promotional tool
- Can be folded away in handbag
- Can be large and good for golfing

Bad points:

- Blows inside out
- Horrid when goes inside – drips everywhere – needs a cover
- Can be difficult to put up

And then take each point and apply that to your own brand or product and ideas will flow for what you can do next.

3. **Reverse idea generation**

Pessimists will love this one! Instead of thinking about how to make the product better, you think about how it could be worse and from that you will get ideas paradoxically to make it better.

Or even take the things that people hate and make them into a marketing story. We end where we began with Marmite – research showed that people were polarised either loving or hating it – this was then made into a marketing positioning that has been here for ten years!

4. **Five whys**

You can use the technique of five whys originated by Japanese industrialist, Sakichi Toyoda, to get to the real reasons why your products are not successful or to identify the opportunities, e.g.

> Why don't people buy bagged salads?
> *Because they end up throwing half away*
> Why do they throw it away?
> *Because the leaves go off*
> Why do the leaves go off?
> *Because the leaves react with air and go off*
> Why do they react with the air?
> *Because the bag is fragile or non resealable*
> Why isn't it resealable?
> *Because it is expensive*

From those five whys you can lift out the opportunities to change the packaging and find a resealable option that is not as expensive.

So, once you have completed your idea generation and come up with the most amazing innovative brand extension idea you may need to fund it, so what are your options?

Sources of funding

I found this amazing infographic on www.jamjarinvestments.com which is the previous Innocent team's innovation business. It sums up funding extremely well.

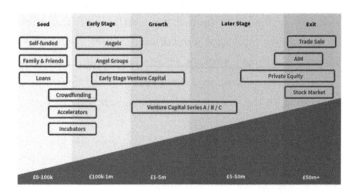

By the time you are at this stage of the book, you are moving into early stage and growth. You may even be thinking about building a new factory! More realistically, you may need funding for a smaller project such as launching new brand, export, etc. I am not an expert in these matters and am merely suggesting ideas – you really do need to get professional advice before you choose your funding path. I know several companies who have come unstuck following the wrong path for investment and losing their company as a result.

You may not need to go externally and can look at reinvestment of profits which is the easiest way to fund the evolution and growth of your business, ensuring you have no dilution of equity, debt or other liability. However, this may not offer you the level of funding that you are seeking and may not enable you to make the step-change of evolution that you know the business is capable of.

Crowdfunding is the popular new way of funding anything from heart operations to publishing a book – although in the end I funded it myself!! Food and drink is the most successful crowdfunding sector with 253 successful campaigns giving an annualised return of 23% (Seedrs 2016). There are a few ways you can approach it depending on the size of investment you are looking for:

1. Rewards – you offer rewards, e.g. free food, etc. in exchange for cash
   * Indiegogo.com
   * Kickstarter.com
2. Equity investment – this is often for bigger, more established businesses with seed capital in place
   * Microventures.com
   * Crowdcube.com
   * Seedrs.com
3. Venture capital offering early-stage funding
   * www.jamjarinvestments.com
   * www.passioncapital.com
   * www.forwardpartners.com

CASE STUDY

The opportunity – Bonnie Chung launched Miso Tasty, a range of Japanese-inspired snacks & meal solutions in 2014. She got national listings in

Waitrose, Sainsbury's, Ocado, Wholefoods, Selfridges, and Harvey Nichols.

Her next milestone was to launch a range of ramen noodle kits into Waitrose in March 2017 but she needed funding to give her the cash flow for stock, promotional support, etc.

The solution – she invested in strong PR getting great coverage and winning awards and was featured in *The Sunday Times, Guardian* and *Independent*, as well as in the foodie press like the *Jamie Oliver Magazine* and won the Award for Japanese Cuisine at 2017 Gourmand World Cookbook Awards.

She then launched a crowdfunding campaign through Seedrs in early spring 2017 primarily to meet the working capital requirement for launching the ramen noodle kits and support the roll-out to other major retailers.

The target to raise was £150k and she smashed this raising £270k funds for 9.5% equity – superb result and a great way to get her business to the next level.

All of these methods need a selling proposition similar to what we did for the retailer in Chapter 7. Investors are looking for profitable businesses that will ultimately be saleable for a significant profit. The details are as follows:

• Product proposition – using the detail from our brand design chapter

- People – who is on the team – use your organisation build from Chapter 10
- Size of prize – what is the market (remember all the work on what market you are in), do you have any intellectual property that will drive the opportunity into other markets, export, etc. and what is your company worth?
- Business plan – what is the route to profitable sales over the next three years
- Investment required – how much money do you want to borrow? What value will the money add to the business?

Other funding options

- Government funding – there are a number of grant opportunities to enable you to evolve and keep ahead of the curve. I have seen businesses build new factories and install energy efficiency equipment such as solar panels and biomass boilers funded by EU/government grant money. SMEs are in a particularly strong position to take advantage of this as the government is keen to encourage this type of enterprise – it depends on your business size, location, etc., etc.
- R&D tax reimbursement – there is a little-known opportunity whereby you can claim back the investment you make in R&D from your tax bill. I would advise you to talk to an expert on this subject but simply put, any investment in genuine R&D, and this is a difficult one to define and why you need the experts, can be offset

against corporation tax. Have a look at www.gov.uk/
guidance/corporation-tax-research-and-development-
rd-relief for more information.

And finally, to sum up everything we have talked about,
I love this infographic from Anna Vital (www.anna.VC):

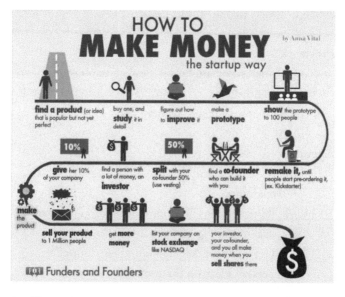

So, if you know where to look, you can step-change your
business to evolve into your dream and ensure that you have
the money to make it happen.

4pm

Exercise

Arrange for a day off site totally free of phone calls, emails, etc. and dedicate it to generating ideas for your future.

Try to have about four to six people in the team either from your own company, factory, packaging supplier, marketing agency, etc. and ensure that you have some creative "ideas" people in that group.

Pre-work
- SWOT analysis of attendees' view of the business
- Each attendee brings a sample of unrelated food product that they feel is inspirational

Agenda

9-10am	Review current understanding of market and customer
10-11am	Random free-flow idea generation session – use samples to generate ideas
11-12pm	Get your packaging/ingredients suppliers to present ideas on the future
12-2pm	Lunch/store visits – preferably go to a new, relevant place for food, e.g. Wholefoods, Selfridges, etc.
2-3pm	Review what you have seen out in the market
3-4pm	Plan your innovation streams for next three years and identify actions, responsibilities and timings. Identify any funding challenges and solutions
	Celebrate!

Epilogue

And, finally... well done for making it to the end of the book!!

It has been an interesting journey for me to write this and interestingly I have learnt so much more about the industry as I have investigated the detail of some of the subjects to ensure that you have a number of interesting examples to read about – some are my personal experiences and some are just interesting industry facts.

But you may now be sitting there saying "OMG, where do I start?" – because it can be overwhelming. Take writing this book – I had loads of ideas and even some chapters already written but it took my book-writing coach, Mindy (see Acknowledgements) to guide me through every step of planning, structuring and reviewing the manuscript and get me ready to publish.

The book may have been enough but just in case you do want a few pointers, if only on where to start – give me a call. Go on my website and schedule an online consultation. Or get in touch – always happy to chat with other food-industry lovers.

Feel free to contact me at karen@foodmentor.co.uk or 00 44 7811 942054

And please let me have feedback on the book and the challenges that you have faced so that when we do the second edition we have new successes – yours – to include as case studies.